PSYCHOLOGICAL
Seduction

D1291020

PSYCHOLOGICAL
Seduction

The Failure of
Modern Psychology

WILLIAM K. KILPATRICK

Roger A. McCaffrey Publishing
Post Office Box 1209 • Ridgefield, CT 06877

Copyright © 1983 by William K. Kilpatrick

All rights reserved. Written permission must be secured from the publisher to use or reproduce any part of this book, except for brief quotations in critical reviews or articles.

Printed in the United States of America

Most of the Scripture quotations in this publication are from the Revised Standard Version of the Bible, copyrighted 1946, 1952, © 1971, 1973 by the Division of Christian Education of the national Council of the Churches of Christ in the U.S.A. and are used by permission.

A few scattered quotations on pages 134, 138, and 146 are from the *Good News Bible*—Old Testament: Copyright © American Bible Society 1976; New Testament: Copyright © American Bible Society 1966, 1971, 1976. The quotation on page 145 is from the New King James Version. Copyright © 1979, 1980, 1982, Thomas Nelson, Inc., Publishers.

Library of Congress Cataloging in Publication Data
Kilpatrick, William Kirk.
 Psychological seduction

 Bibliography: p.239
 1. Christianity—Psychology—Controversial literature
1: Title
BR110.K48   1983
ISBN 0-9661325-0-5

To Kathleen

CONTENTS

PREFACE

Psychology is a river with many branches and tributaries. This book is not intended to explore every branch but to chart the general direction and force of the stream. The criticisms I offer in the pages that follow are directed toward psychology as a social force: in other words, psychology as it influences our everyday ways of thinking and acting. Psychology as a science has a legitimate part to play in our society. It is another matter, however, when it wants to play every part and direct the drama as well. What I have to say in the following chapters does not apply equally to all areas of psychology; but rather than make constant qualifications ("this, but not that"), I have used, for the most part, the simple word *psychology*.

psychological
seduction

CHAPTER 1

Wolf in the Fold

The deep faith we have in psychology was illustrated for me while attending church in Scotland a few years ago. The incident was not dramatic, but it has stuck in my mind. The priest was delivering a sermon, and to buttress his message he referred to the authority of John's Gospel, the Epistles of Saint Paul, the writings of Saint Augustine, and so on. The congregation seemed unmoved. The man to my left yawned. A woman in the next row was checking the contents of her purse.

"As Erich Fromm says. . . ," the priest continued. Instantly a visible stir of attention rippled through the crowd as it strained forward to catch every nuance. The yawning man closed his mouth, and the lady shut her purse; both came alert. Erich Fromm. Of course! If anyone knew the answers to the riddles of life, it would be Erich Fromm.

It seemed two kinds of faith prevailed in that congregation: faith in God and faith in psychology. It was hard to say which was the higher faith. But I doubt anyone there would have thought of it in terms of two different faiths. The real problem is telling them apart at all.

In fact, when people hear I'm involved with both psychology and Christianity, they generally assume I'm working on a synthesis to bring the two closer together, to patch up whatever few remaining differences there might be. "Aren't psychology and religion just two different ways of getting at the same thing?"—it's a question I often hear.

It is true that popular psychology shares much in common with Eastern religion; in fact, a merger is well under way. But if you're talking about Christianity, it is much truer to say that psychology and religion are competing faiths. If you seriously hold to one set of values, you will logically have to reject the other.

The Gospel of Self-esteem

For the time being, however, confusion seems to have the upper hand. For instance, I know of a priest in one Catholic church who tells his congregation, "The purpose of Christ's coming was to say, 'You're O.K., and I'm O.K.'" In other churches parents are told that their children are incapable of sinning because "that's what psychologists tell us." In many evangelical churches, positive thinking seems to have taken the place of faith. Almost everywhere, salvation is becoming equated with self-growth or feelings of O.K.-ness. In short, Christians have let their faith become tangled in a net of popular ideas about self-esteem and self-fulfillment that aren't Christian at all.

The present situation reminds me of some advice on temptation given by an old devil to his demon nephew. In C. S. Lewis's classic book, *The Screwtape Letters,* Screwtape instructs Wormwood to keep his man confused: "Keep his mind off the plain antithesis between True and False"; and keep him "in the state of mind I call 'Christianity and.' You know—Christianity and the Crisis, Christianity and the New Psychology, Christianity and the New Order. . . ."

Christianity and the New Psychology. . . . Lewis was more prophetic than he could have guessed. What was only a minor confusion in 1941 has turned into mass confusion. It is difficult to say any longer where psychology leaves off and Christianity begins.

For non-Christians, popular psychology has an equally seductive influence. Many seem to turn to it as a substitute for traditional faiths. They may even think of it as a more evolved form of religion—a more efficient and compassionate way of doing good than Christianity. Psychology levels the hills of anxiety and makes the crooked way straight. It is the rod and staff that comforts them.

Psychology's Appeal: Counterfeit Christianity

The appeal psychology has for both Christians and non-Christians is a complex one. But it is difficult to make sense of it at all unless you understand that it is basically a religious appeal. For the truth is, psychology bears a surface resemblance to Christianity.

Not doctrinal Christianity, of course. Most psychologists are hostile to that. And naturally enough, so are non-Christians. Nevertheless, there is a certain Christian tone to what psychology says and does: echoes of loving your neighbor as yourself, the promise of being made whole, avoidance of judging others. Those ideas are appealing to most people, no matter what their faith.

But like most counterfeits, popular psychology does not deliver on its promises. Instead, it leads both Christians and non-Christians away from duty or proper conduct. It is a seduction in the true sense of the word.

One task of this book, then, is to disentangle Christianity from the psychological religion. Once we have done that, I think it will be seen that Christianity is and has been all along a better way of meeting our needs—even those needs that are usually thought of as purely human. In short, although

Christianity is more than a psychology, it happens to be better psychology than psychology is.

A Personal Note

But before I continue, I should first admit that I, too, was a victim of the confusion between psychology and Christianity. My own experience may help to illustrate how it can come about.

I began to lose interest in the Christian faith in graduate school. That was when I discovered psychology. I didn't realize I was losing interest in Christianity; I merely thought I was adding something on. But before long I had shifted my faith from the one to the other.

There was no reason not to. As far as I could see, there was no essential difference between the two. I had been reading the most liberal theologians—that is to say, the most psychologized ones—and from what I could gather, the important thing in religion was not Bible or creed but simply loving other people. I thought I could swing that easily enough without the help of church or prayers. Such practices, I assumed, were intended for those who hadn't attained awareness.

Freud had been astonished by the biblical commandment "Love thy neighbor." "How can it be possible?" he asked. I thought it would be easy. The modern psychologists seemed to be on my side. Moreover, they seemed in agreement with the modern theologians: both could approvingly quote Augustine's "Love and do what you will."

Psychology, in addition, had interesting explanations for almost every type of human behavior, and I had no reason to doubt its version. Erich Fromm said that to love others you first have to love yourself. Didn't that square with what Jesus taught? It certainly made wonderful sense to me; like most other twenty-two-year-olds, I thoroughly loved myself. My newfound Bible was psychologist Carl Rogers's *On Becoming a Person*. In it Rogers gently suggested that humans are at heart good and decent creatures with no more natural disposition toward hatred than a rosebud. I looked within and found no hate. There were no bad people, I concluded, only bad environments.

Rogers's optimistic doctrine coincided with the religious trend of those days. Intellectuals in the church were downplaying sin as though it were an accidental holdover from the Middle Ages. In explaining the scanty attention given to moral evil in his book *The Divine Milieu*, the priest-paleontologist Pierre Teilhard de Chardin observed that "the soul with which we are dealing is assumed to have already turned away from the path of error." In less solemn language, an acquaintance of mine, a priest, declared that children should not be taught the Ten Commandments. It was bad psychology, he said.

I had no reason to doubt other prevalent ideas in psychology. Abraham Maslow, whose photograph and books seemed to glow with good-hearted wisdom, said that "B-love" (from the fullness of your being) was good and "D-love" (out of a need or deficit) was bad. In those days, I didn't realize how needy I was, or how large my inner deficit. I was already half-convinced that a healthy person didn't really need others.

Healthy people never felt revenge, either. Erich Fromm explained that the productive person does not desire to get even. Only the crippled and impotent do so—people like Hitler. I pitied them, those crippled, impotent revenge-seekers. If only they could learn to love—like Erich Fromm and I. My own experience with revenge up to that time had been a few childhood grudges that hadn't lasted more than a day or so. I had no notion of its power to make dust and ashes

[17]

of the productive life. I was unaware that a person could yearn for vengeance the way a vampire thirsts after blood. The idea that revenge might actually seem sweet—something so compelling that the biblical prophets warned constantly against it—was beyond my comprehension. It shouldn't have been, of course. I had thrilled to Ulysses' revenge on the suitors, and I enjoyed revenge movies immensely. As in many other areas, I was blissfully unaware of the discrepancy between my psychological precepts and my actual experience.

I was also unaware of the growing discrepancy between my psychological creed and my religious one. The fact that such a discrepancy existed was muffled by the noise of many clerical voices lifted in praise of psychology. A priest introduced me to the writings of Carl Rogers, and a minister suggested I read Maslow and Fromm. Other priests and ministers were introducing encounter-type activities into church services.

My personal introduction to the world of encounter, and to other expressions of humanistic psychology, was through a minister. Once he invited me to a party given in his honor by students who had taken his workshop in human sexuality. When I arrived, the celebrants had already divided into standing circles of six or seven. Almost as soon as I walked into the house, an arm snaked out from one of these circles and pulled me in.

"What's your name?" someone said.

I told him.

"We love you," he said, and the others murmured, "We love you," as we rocked gently back and forth, arm around shoulder. I felt nothing—some sort of deficiency in my nature, I guessed—but I lowered my head anyway and made a murmuring noise.

Meanwhile, I had developed a mental habit of seeing

harmony in all things. I was fond of the phrase "all knowledge is one." I sought synthesis everywhere. Religious, philosophical, psychological, and sociological ideas blended easily and conveniently. Maslow's thoughts merged with those of the Jewish theologian Martin Buber in one tributary of my mind, splashed over whatever sluice gates stood in the way, and joined with numerous other tributaries, swirling together toward oceanic oneness.

Soon I began to blur other lines: those that separated good and evil. It was possible, I found, to transmute good into evil and evil into good by minor adjustments in definition: the loosening of a spring here, the turning of a spindle there. But it was hardly necessary to do so. My consciousness of sin was at a low ebb—the result, no doubt, of a habit of almost total self-acceptance. I had learned to trust my instincts; if I desired something, it must be good. It was hard to see how I could go wrong as long as I was true to my desires and strove for self-fulfillment.

I became convinced, despite years of Christian training to the contrary, that evil was not a thing that inhered in people but rather was the result of unjust social conditions and bad environments. My own basic instincts were, I felt, noble and decent. My intention was that all people should grow together in peace, brotherhood, and charity. If society had failed to reach this harmony, that was mainly because individuals had not learned to love themselves. As a teacher I saw an opportunity to remedy this lack of self-love. I would supply the empathy and unconditional acceptance I assumed my students were not getting from their psychologically unsophisticated parents. There would be no Hitlers or Stalins coming out of my classes.

In all this—this "maturation" process—I saw no need for sacrifice or hard choices. I felt no need to renounce cherished beliefs. They simply melted away like March snowmen. More often than not, the melting-away process was aided and abetted by theologians who were eager to remove difficult parts of the faith. Anything that might separate one from the world was considered a fair target. Before long, however, it was the world that had my allegiance. As a child I had been deeply moved and delighted to be a member of the church. But like the child of immigrant parents, ashamed of their accent and anxious to assimilate, I had now arrived at a stage of life where I would have been deeply embarrassed just to be associated with it. It would have been awkward all around. I was now prepared to abandon most of my Christian heritage to the realm of mythology or antiquity, and adopt in its place the new streamlined beliefs that talked very little about anything except love.

Perhaps I am giving a wrong impression here. The Christian faith is a very strong thing. It won't let you off that easily. Some core elements of my faith did remain. There were places beyond which I could not, would not retreat. Certain of my beliefs would not be budged. But where this was the case, I simply failed to admit the possibility of any contradiction with my cherished psychological beliefs. I liked A and I liked B, and I was sure they would like each other once they met. I admired psychologists for their spirituality, and I admired theologians for their psychological awareness. There could be no possibility of a quarrel between them.

Whatever reconciliation I managed to effect between psychology and Christianity, however, was always at the expense of Christianity. The Christian view of life that had once powerfully pervaded my thinking was continually crumbling at the edges, leaving a smaller and smaller center.

As the Christian sphere shrank, the humanist sphere enlarged. I was, in modern parlance, "learning a lot about myself." I found that I could make more allowance for myself than I had previously thought possible. Any inner tendency that I might previously have restrained, I now welcomed with open arms as an old friend. I was learning to accept myself. And the liberality that I extended to myself, I extended to others in a positive debauch of tolerance. I believed that I and the rest of humanity were on the threshold of deeper and more wonderful discoveries about the self. One only had to learn to let go, to float free on the stream of instinct.

It was an exciting time. I was associating with people who not only felt the same as I did but also seemed far advanced in the art of living, people who by anybody's criteria were *exciting*. Our conversations were exhilarating, daring, elevated out of the ordinary. Or so I thought. When I was with these companions, I felt as though we made up a secret society, a brilliant gnostic sect surrounded by gray orthodoxy.

We didn't have a motto, but if we had, I think it would have been "Why not?"

But no. I never went to the extreme of making a full-blown religion out of psychology. Something in my early Christian training prevented me. In addition, events in my life were beginning to undermine my easy confidence in the possibility of self-salvation.

There had been no reason to question psychological explanations of life because, until my late twenties, my life had been packed in cotton wool. Now, a series of events unfolded for which my psychological expertise had not prepared me. Although the problems I encountered were not much different from those facing most adults, the idea had somehow seeped into my mind that they wouldn't happen to a self-actualizing person. Between the lines, the psychologists whom I most admired seemed to hint that suffering was not the common lot of humanity but some kind of foolish mistake that could be avoided by a better understanding of human dynamics.

I was making a lot of foolish mistakes. My best intentions reaped the worst consequences. My best efforts brought failure—not always, but often enough to put large dents in my plans for self-actualization. One dream, it seemed, could only be purchased at the price of another. Moreover, I discovered that though I had no appetite for sacrifice or hardship, they were required of anyone wishing to maintain a bare minimum of responsibility. Meanwhile, my experiments in self-expression were getting me into unpleasant situations and forcing me to reconsider my faith in my own essential innocence.

My life was getting out of hand, and the only advice I could get from psychologist friends was to open up more. At this point, there was nothing left to open up. Openness surrounded me on all sides, like a pit.

A reverse process set in. My faith in psychology began, though slowly, to disintegrate. I had put some weight on the psychological scaffold, and it had given way. I still repeated the stock formulas (I was by now teaching psychology), but it was fast becoming apparent that most of it no longer applied to my own life. My life could only appear ridiculous by the commonly accepted standards of self-growth. In terms of self-development, as it was then popularly understood, I was on the road to regression. It was foolishness. And there is no place for being a fool in the psychological system.

But there was elsewhere—in the faith I had ignored for over a decade while remaining open to meaning everywhere else. A well-established Christian tradition held that what appeared as foolishness in the eyes of men did not necessar-

ily appear so in the eyes of God. Perhaps that ancient promise warranted another look.

I did come back to Christianity—real Christianity, not the
diluted version. It was a slow return: so slow and reluctant
that I would be foolish to hold myself up as any sort of model
for imitation. The point I wish to make here is that religion
and psychology had become nearly indistinguishable for
me. Freud and the church fathers, faith in God and faith in
human potential, revelation and self-revelation—all slid together in an easy companionship. As for God, He began to
take shape in my mind along the lines of a friendly counselor
of the nondirective school. I never balked at doing His will.
His will always coincided with my own.

The Wolf in Sheep's Clothing

True Christianity does not mix well with psychology.
When you try to mix them, you often end up with a
watered-down Christianity instead of a Christianized
psychology. But the process is subtle and is rarely noticed. I
wasn't aware that I was confusing two different things. And
others in the church who might have been expected to put
me right were under the same enchantment as I. It was not a
frontal attack on Christianity—I'm sure I would have re-
sisted that. It was not a case of a wolf at the door: the wolf was
already in the fold, dressed in sheep's clothing. And from
the way it was petted and fed by some of the shepherds, one
would think it was the prize sheep.

What happened to me was not unusual.

During the late sixties and through the seventies a new
climate of psychological ideas settled over Catholic and liberal Protestant congregations. Many of the clergy, nuns, and
lay leaders began, out of good intentions, to mix their faith

with sociology, psychology, and secular causes. At the same time, many of them elevated personal development to a place all out of proportion to spiritual development. Their faith eventually became so thinned out with admixtures that it was no longer strong enough to sustain them when a personal or social crisis struck. Thousands left the church. When asked in a survey why they had left, one population of former nuns checked off "inability to be me" as the main reason. The faith of the average believer was also shaken. Some stuck it out. Some turned away altogether from their faith. Others joined Christian churches that seemed more certain and unconfused.

Has the problem abated? Not at all. The new hybrid religion seems to grow stronger.

A friend of mine recently asked a Sunday school teacher about the course emphasis and was told, "We are teaching the children to grow, to become whole persons, to question, to choose values." Another, a nun, simply said, "We are showing them how to become whole persons." The first woman ordained as a priest by the Episcopal church was asked by an interviewer if she considered herself to be a woman of strong religious faith. She replied that, no, she did not, "but I do believe in caring, and that's what religion is all about, isn't it?" At a gathering of Harvard Divinity School scholars I talked to a professor who preferred the newly discovered "gnostic gospels" to the Gospels of Matthew, Mark, Luke, and John because the "masculine" Gospels "didn't meet the needs of women."

Nor is this purely a Catholic or liberal phenomenon. Evangelical and charismatic Christians have unguarded borders where psychological ideas easily slip over. Some of the media evangelists preach a gospel of personal mastery and success that has very little to do with Scripture and a great deal to do with positive thinking—although nowadays I believe it is called "possibility thinking." At the back of this is the idea that faith will lead to healthy personality, a cure for disease, and even to financial security. In these cases it is sometimes not at all clear whether we are to believe in God or in ourselves.

Rather than taking a lesson from the sad experience of the Catholics, some evangelicals seem bent on making the same mistakes. A recent book by a renowned evangelical minister calls for a "new reformation" based on self-esteem, which he calls "the highest value." In this "emerging reformation," says the author, psychology and theology will "work side by side as strong allies."

No one who reads this man can doubt his good intentions and his bright hopes. But anyone who can read the recent past and see the result of such alliances will not be so optimistic.

"Christianity And"

These attempts to make common cause with psychology are examples of "Christianity And." It's a strong temptation to those who fear that Christianity by itself isn't enough. The trouble is that "Christianity And" edges real Christianity aside or prevents it from taking hold.

Lewis once suggested that we imagine Christianity as a good disease: something you want to catch. In that case, "Christianity And" is like an innoculation. It's a small dose of the real thing mixed up with other serums. It might give you a bump on the arm or a mild fever, but it prevents you from getting the good infection that you ought to be getting. Of course, the most harmful effects of this process will be on young people who have been exposed to nothing else.

A Concern for All

Now, it is obvious why Christians should be concerned about the lure of psychology. But why should non-Christians care?

Only because they and their children also live in the psychological society. And if it is true that Christians have been led away from their faith by psychology, it seems to me equally true that we have all been led away from our better instincts and common sense. We can ask of certain psychological claims, "Are they irreligious?" But we can also ask, "Are they realistic?" If there are flaws in the system, they will crop up in practical matters, in which case they will offend not only the gods but our sense of logic as well.

This brings us to a final point. The average man is no longer scared to hear that his behavior may lead to hell, but he thinks twice if he hears that it will lead to the state hospital. I am not saying that we are all on the road to the madhouse—although a case can be made for that position—but I am suggesting that we are all being edged closer to the kind of bleak and colorless life that the state hospital represents. An overserious attitude toward the self is an unhealthy and ultimately defeating preoccupation. It leads not to a society of different and interesting individuals but to a drab hive of look-alikes and talk-alikes droning the same stories, buzzing with self-concern.

The point I am getting at is this. Even in purely worldly terms there is no certainty that psychological ideas make us any better off. We have tons of expert advice, plus mountains of revelations about the self. Do we step more lightly or laugh more heartily because of it?

Being a Christian, then, is not a requirement for following the arguments of this book. The criticism I make is offered on intellectual grounds as well as spiritual ones. Psychology wants us to judge an idea not on whether it will save a man's soul but on whether it will save his sanity. Its goal is to make life more human. It can be demonstrated, I believe, that psychology has rather less to contribute to that goal than is commonly thought and that Christianity has rather more.

CHAPTER 2

Good Intentions

If you take your car to a garage for repairs and find afterwards that it still doesn't work correctly and has developed additional complications as well, you will be inclined to be suspicious. If it happens repeatedly, you will stop going to that garage. You won't necessarily be suspicious about the ethics of the repairman. Perhaps you know him to be a good man. But you will wonder about his competence.

There is no reason either to doubt the generous impulse behind the work of professional psychologists and social scientists. Most of the experts who guide the psychological society have good intentions. We can go further and say that many are dedicated and self-sacrificing. Counselors and therapists often supply the care and concern that desperate individuals can find in no other quarter. And most psychological research is aimed at the ultimate betterment of the race.

But there may be reasons to doubt the competence of psychological helpers. A willingness to help does not guarantee a helpful result. Sometimes, as Thoreau wryly observed, the result is the opposite: "If I knew for a certainty that a man was coming to my house with the conscious design of doing me good, I should run for my life."

Do Psychologists Know How to Help?

The fact that psychologists are trying to help people often

keeps us from asking whether they know how to help. We think it's bad manners to ask a man who is trying to help us if he really knows what he's doing. Of course, it's not just manners that prevent us from questioning psychology. It's also faith—the kind of faith that makes us believe that school teachers are doing what is best for our children. Or the kind of faith that tells you that the man in the clerical collar won't knock you down and steal your wallet. Just the same, we ought to be asking if psychologists really do know how to help. A good deal of research suggests that psychology is ineffective. And there is evidence pointing to the conclusion that psychology is actually harmful.

The first indication that psychology might be ineffective came in 1952 when Hans Eysenck of the Institute of Psychiatry, University of London, discovered that neurotic people who do not receive therapy are as likely to recover as those who do. Psychotherapy, he found, was not any more effective than the simple passage of time. Additional studies by other researchers showed similar results. Then Dr. Eugene Levitt of the Indiana University School of Medicine found that disturbed children who were not treated recovered at the same rate as disturbed children who were. A further indication of the problem was revealed in the results of the extensive Cambridge-Somerville Youth Study. The researchers found that uncounseled juvenile delinquents had a lower rate of further trouble than counseled ones. Other studies have shown that untrained lay people do as well as psychiatrists or clinical psychologists in treating patients. And the Rosenham studies indicated that mental hospital staff could not even tell normal people from genuinely disturbed ones. It is possible to go on with the list. It is quite a long one. But I hope this is sufficient to make the point that when psychologists rush in to help, they are not particularly successful.

Psychological Values and Traditional Values

There is a further point, a more serious charge. Psychology and other social sciences might be doing actual harm to our society. It is not just a case of what this or that therapist does. This particular therapist may be a godsend to his clients. The point is that on a larger scale psychological values have run roughshod over traditional ones. And there are reasons to think there is something destructive about the new values.

You needn't be a scholar to sense this. In fact, scholarship is often a hindrance to understanding what is really happening. An average parent or a factory laborer is more likely than the professor to catch on when something goes wrong with society. Many parents now feel themselves to be in the position of helpless spectators watching their children nurtured on alien values at school or through the media. The old stories about fairies and witches who stole children away at night and replaced them with changelings seem strangely contemporary.

A rather blatant example of this body snatching comes from Sweden, perhaps the most therapeutically oriented country in the world, where a law has been passed forbidding parents to spank their children. Further, it is a criminal offense to threaten, ostracize, ridicule, or otherwise "psychologically abuse" children. Presumably this means that parents can no longer raise their voices at their children or send them to their rooms. But there is no evidence that the Swedes are any less melancholy for this enlightenment. By all reports the young people are more bored and restless than ever.

The Failure of the Psychological Faith

However good-intentioned and however nice, it is not at

all clear that the psychological establishment knows how to help. Everywhere there are dark hints that the faith doesn't work. Despite the creation of a virtual army of psychiatrists, psychologists, psychometrists, counselors, and social workers, there has been no letup in the rate of mental illness, suicide, alcoholism, drug addiction, child abuse, divorce, murder, and general mayhem. Contrary to what one might expect in a society so carefully analyzed and attended to by mental health experts, there has been an increase in all these categories. It sometimes seems there is a direct ratio between the increasing number of helpers and the increasing number of those who need help. The more psychologists we have, the more mental illness we get; the more social workers and probation officers, the more crime; the more teachers, the more ignorance.

One has to wonder at it all. In plain language, it is suspicious. We are forced to entertain the possibility that psychology and related professions are proposing to solve problems that they themselves have helped to create. We find psychologists raising people's expectations for happiness in this life to an inordinate level, and then we find them dispensing advice about the mid-life crisis and dying. We find psychologists making a virtue out of self-preoccupation, and then we find them surprised at the increased supply of narcissists. We find psychologists advising the courts that there is no such thing as a bad boy or even a bad adult, and then we find them formulating theories to explain the rise in crime. We find psychologists severing the bonds of family life, and then we find them conducting therapy for broken families.

Expectations and Results

There are too many "ifs," "ands," and "buts" to prove a causal connection between the rise of psychology and the deterioration of the social bond, but there is certainly enough evidence to make doubtful the claim that psychology benefits us. In areas where professionals really do know what they are doing, we expect that it will show. Stanislav Andreski, a British sociologist, makes that point clear in comparing psychology and sociology to other professions. He notes that when a profession is based on well-established knowledge, there ought to be a connection between the number of practitioners and the results achieved:

> Thus, in a country which has an abundance of telecommunication engineers, the provision of telephonic facilities will normally be better than in a country which has only a few specialists of this kind. The levels of mortality will be lower in countries or regions where there are many doctors and nurses than in places where they are few and far between. Accounts will be more generally and efficiently kept in countries with many trained accountants than where they are scarce.[1]

And what are the benefits produced by psychology and sociology? Professor Andreski continues:

> . . . So, we should find that in countries, regions, institutions or sectors where the services of psychologists are widely used, families are more enduring, bonds between the spouses, siblings, parents and children stronger and warmer, relations between colleagues more harmonious, the treatment of recipients of aid better, vandals, criminals and drug addicts fewer, than in places or groups which do not avail themselves of the psychologists' skills. On this basis we could infer that the blessed country of harmony and peace is of course the United States; and that it ought to have been becoming more and more so during the last quarter of the century in step with the growth in numbers of sociologists, psychologists, and political scientists.[2]

But this is not what has happened. On the contrary, things appear to be getting worse. Streets are unsafe. Families are in tatters. Suicide cuts off young lives. And when the psychological society attempts to deal with such problems, it often seems to make them worse. The introduction of suicide prevention centers in cities, for instance, is followed by a rise of suicide. Marriage counseling often leads to divorce. And commonsense observation tells us that the introduction of widespread public sex education has done nothing to check the increase of unwanted pregnancies, promiscuity, and venereal disease. There is evidence, rather, that such programs encourage premature sexuality with its attendant problems.

It is difficult to avoid the conclusion that the prescription may be causing the disease. "If we saw," wrote Andreski, "that whenever a fire brigade comes, the flames become even fiercer, we might well begin to wonder what it is that they are squirting, and whether they are not by any chance pouring oil on to the fire."[3]

Research and Common Sense

Here a caution is in order. Although the case against psychology is strong, I don't want to leave the impression that there is conclusive proof of psychology's failure. Statistical evidence always has its problems. For instance, the fact that two things occur together is no proof that one causes the other. If a rise in crime happens to be accompanied by a rise in the stock market, we couldn't conclude that a rising market causes crime. The fact that the growth of psychology corresponds to growing social problems could conceivably be only a coincidence. One could even argue that these problems might be much worse had not psychology been around to help. Finally, one could admit that there have been failures, but argue that the basic ideas are sound even if they've been misapplied.

We have a much better case, I believe, when these ideas are checked against our experience or our common sense.

Take, for example, two of the most tenaciously held claims of popular psychology: the idea that role-playing stunts our self-expression and the idea that venting anger is good for us. If you subject either of these notions to a moment's reflection, you will see there are a great many instances where the reverse is true.

Suppose, for example, that an elementary school teacher is reading a story to her class. Suppose further that it is a story full of power, emotion, and noble sentiments. Now suppose she is so moved that she feels like crying. Should she give in to her feelings? Should she allow herself to break down in a fit of sobbing? At the moment that might well be the "natural" thing to do. But I think we would agree that the better thing is for her to pull herself together and continue with the story, giving it the best dramatic reading she can. The alternative is that the students lose out on what the story has to offer. After all, she has read it before, and it is now their turn to benefit from its power. Let *them* cry. Indeed, let them weep hot tears, but do not put them in the confused and embarrassed position of having to comfort an adult who cannot play her role.

Does role-playing hamper self-expression? Perhaps sometimes it does. But sometimes self-expression can get in the way of deeper, more forceful expression. And on those occasions, playing our roles well is the most human and authentic thing we can do.

As for the idea that expressing anger gets rid of it, think about the people you know who are most free in indulging their anger. Isn't it usually the case that their hostility simply escalates? The expression of hostility, as anyone can readily observe, often perpetuates and increases anger.

Psychologists themselves are now coming around to this view. A new book on the subject of anger concludes that letting off steam is generally bad for us. The book happens to be stocked with research evidence to prove the point. But should we be spending our lives waiting for the scientific verdict on things we can see with our own two eyes?

The chapter ahead will give us a chance to check out one of the more popular current notions, examining it both in the light of faith and in the light of common sense.

CHAPTER 3

Self-esteem

"It's important to like yourself."

"If you don't like yourself, nobody else will."

"Jimmy's problem is his poor self-concept."

How many times have we heard these or similar sentiments? The taxi driver is as likely to express them as the teacher, the plumber as readily as the psychologist. In fact, we're all pretty much convinced that self-esteem is the key to any number of problems.

This business of liking oneself has become for us almost a first principle. It seems self-evident, in the same category with "the sky is blue." No one is inclined to dispute it. Psychology, of course, didn't invent the notion, but it has capitalized on it. You might say it is the "good news" of the psychological gospel.

So when I undertake to criticize the idea of self-esteem, it is with trepidation. It is like criticizing the proposition "babies are lovable." Nevertheless, the idea does require a closer look, because ideas, like dinnerware, usually come in sets, and some of the notions that accompany the faith in self-esteem are not so charming as little babies.

Self-help books, for example, will often start off by asking you to love yourself, but before long they are telling you you're not responsible for other people and that you shouldn't waste time living up to others' expectations. Most of us know also that "feeling good about myself" is sometimes a handy excuse for doing self-centered or even selfish things. We say, "I won't be much good to others if I'm not good to myself," and the next thing we do is send our three-year-old off to daycare for fifty hours a week or dip into family funds so we can take a day at the races.

Our response to the question "Should you like yourself?" has to be tempered with common sense. Our answer should be "That depends" or "Under what circumstances?" All of us, I take it, would like to see the self-rejecting teen-ager who frets over her popularity learn to relax and accept herself. The main question, I suppose, is should she continue to like herself when she is spreading vicious rumors or when she callously manipulates others to improve her social standing. Are we, in other words, to like ourselves regardless of how we behave?

How the Christian View Differs

Now the psychological answer to this question is to say that if we truly like ourselves these other things won't happen—or they won't happen as much. According to this view, people who realize their self-worth don't have any need to do ugly or unkind things. And this is the point, please note, where Christianity and psychology part company. People will continue to behave badly, says the Christian, because human nature is twisted, and liking yourself doesn't remove the twist. But psychological theory doesn't take account of the Fall; it takes the position that there are no bad natural inclinations. As a consequence there is no reason we shouldn't accept ourselves as we are.

Although, as I say, this is a point of conflict between Christianity and psychology, some Christians do not see it as such because, at first glance, the psychological view and the Christian one seem to correspond. Christianity also tells us we ought to love ourselves but for an entirely different reason: because God loves us. We are not centers of wholeness and goodness all by ourselves. We are of infinite worth because we are the apple of God's eye. He loves us as a mother loves her child.

Perhaps, however, it is more accurate to say "as a mother loves her *disobedient* child," for love in that case will want to apply the proper correction. This is the point that some Christians forget. All they see is the similarity: Christianity says we are of great worth, and so does psychology. From there they jump to the conclusion that Christians could profit from listening to psychology's newer insights about self-love. They think they are doing the Christian world a favor, but in fact they are doing it and themselves a disservice by confusing two opposing concepts. Usually they end up taking a view toward themselves and toward God that owes more to psychology than it does to religion. They picture God as an understanding therapist, who only wants us to come to love and accept ourselves for what we are. Rather than accept such a watered-down view of God, we would do well to remember T. S. Eliot's image of Christ as "the wounded surgeon" who performs radical surgery on us because what we need is not a pat on the back but an operation: very possibly a heart transplant.

Something to Feel Good About

Christianity wants you to feel good about yourself, but not until there is something to feel good about. It would like to get us on the road to recovery before it congratulates us on our good health. This, as C. S. Lewis points out, is the mark of someone who really cares for you: "It is for people whom we care nothing about that we demand happiness on any terms: with our friends, our lovers, our children, we are

[38]

more exacting and would rather see them suffer much than be happy in contemptible and estranging modes."[1] A father or mother would leave much to be desired who could say, "It doesn't matter what kind of person my daughter is or what she does as long as she feels good about herself." We would have to wonder how strong that parent's love is. When you love someone, you don't like to see them do unlovely things. You want to make them more lovable. We should expect nothing less from a loving God. And if we are interested in joining the community of saints, we should not expect the invitation to read, "Come as you are; we don't want to change you" (which, by the way, is a radio ad for the Unitarian church).

The reason Christians have to be careful about mixing these two views of self-esteem is because the psychological perspective reduces the good news of the gospel to the status of "nice news"—"nice" because there was never any bad news in the first place. If psychology's great optimism about raw human nature is correct, then Christianity is not necessary: Christ's redemptive action on the cross becomes superfluous. After all, why should He have suffered and died to redeem us if there is nothing wrong with us? If all we need do to find wholeness is just be ourselves, then His death sums up to a meaningless gesture, a noble but unneeded self-sacrifice.

Clearly then, Christians cannot accept the doctrine of natural goodness implied in most theories of self-esteem. The question is why anyone would want to accept it. It is worth noting that Freud himself did not believe it. He believed something quite the opposite: "Man is a wolf to man," he observed in *Civilization and Its Discontents*. Yet his opinion on this matter is largely ignored or evaded today. We prefer to keep our faith in human nature. But the claim for human goodness requires much faith. And that for the very good reason that it is denied at every turn by certain well-known facts: crime statistics, terrorism, war, slavery, concentration camps, brutal parents, ungrateful children, the meanness of everyday behavior. G. K. Chesterton once observed that the doctrine of fallen man is the only Christian belief for which there is overwhelming empirical evidence.

The truth is, though, that statistics don't often convince us. If I thought they did, I would mention some important psychological experiments that contradict the notion of natural goodness. It seems more useful, however, to bring the matter to a more personal level, that is, to the level on which common experience speaks its piece.

Now self-awareness will reveal some pleasant facts about ourselves, but it will also reveal some that aren't so pleasant. My impression is that much of the "evidence" for our goodness is based not on what we actually do but on what we think we would do in this or that situation or on what we believe people ought to do. We all talk a better game than we play. We know exactly what we would do if we were the quarterback on the field, but the truth is, given the chance, we would fumble far more often than he does.

We all say, for example, that it's wrong to treat people as objects. Yet we do it every day. We get this bit of useful information out of X, or that small favor out of Y, and then we are done with them. It wouldn't matter to us if we didn't see them for another month or until they might prove useful again. Or think how we react upon hearing of a flaw in a good man's life. Isn't it true that we are often secretly pleased to find there is less goodness than was supposed? If you are tempted to reply "that's just human nature," remember that it is precisely human nature that is at issue here.

There are worse things, of course, known usually only to us: deeds over which we've held our breath, hoping they wouldn't be discovered—and ready with a pack of lies in case they were. There are other deeds we've never dared look at squarely: things we quickly plastered over with excuses, telling ourselves we had no other choice when in fact we did; avoiding any real examination of our behavior because we knew it could never stand up to such a test. Rather than preventing such behavior, self-esteem often encourages it. It lets us think we are entitled to waive the rules because we are a special kind.

I know in my own case that the most shameful incidents of my life—things I now wince to think about—were the product of a happy self-acceptance, the period during which I was most smitten with self-esteem, "innocently" following what I had convinced myself were good or at least neutral impulses. My self-esteem simply wouldn't allow any honest self-awareness: that only came much later.

When we manage, however briefly and vaguely, to bring to mind our mean and tawdry acts, it is, of course, only half the story. The other half is made up of the things we haven't done but would do if we thought we could get away with them: the things we are tempted to do in the anonymity of a strange city or in the company of people with whom we do not ordinarily associate. We avoid those things because we are afraid of being caught and disgraced, or even sent to jail.

The truth is that the law and the fear of public censure keep us good more times than we care to admit. "Every man," wrote Lewis, ". . . has to 'live up to' the outward appearance of other men: he knows there is that within him which falls far below even his most careless public behavior, even his loosest talk." And no one else could guess, said Lewis, "how familiar and, in a sense, congenial to your soul these things were, how much of a piece with all the rest."[2]

If you bring up these points to the humanist, he may retreat a step or two, but he won't change his direction. His next argument is likely to be something like this: "You've missed the point," he will say. "When someone goes wrong it's not he that's at fault, it's his culture." He claims, in other words, that society won't allow people to be themselves; it warps their good impulses. So if you want to see what the real self is like, you must find people who haven't been twisted by society—young children, for instance. Now this, it must be admitted, is good advice. If you take it, the first thing you discover is that the humanists haven't looked very closely at children: they are not as a rule a good advertisement for the natural state.

To test this, imagine yourself suddenly deposited in a land of giants and then consider whether you would prefer to be discovered by a group of four-year-old giants or a group of adult giants. If, for romantic reasons, you are inclined toward the four-year-olds, think about the chancy fortunes of your family cat when he is with the younger set. Then think of his much more certain chance of being treated humanely by adults. Children are undeniably charming, but they are also an example of how badly we need society if we are not to be ruled by power, whim, and selfishness. The business of snatching toys, refusing to share, hitting little sisters, and lying outrageously to cover it all up begins early enough in the child's life to suggest that the fatal flaw lies not in his society but in his nature. It is society, after all, acting through the parent, that teaches him to return the stolen wagon, to share his playthings, to treat his sister nicely, and to tell the truth. To have missed all this does not speak very well for the observational powers of those who preach natural goodness.

The Weakness of the Psychological Position

Should we love ourselves? Yes, we should. But once you remove the Christian rationale for self-love, it is difficult to see on what other grounds it might be based. If you look at the psychological rationale, you can see how very thin it is. It usually goes like this: "Self-love means accepting yourself as a worthy person because you choose to do so." Or, "You exist; you are human. That is all you need. Your worth is determined by you." Or simply, "You are worthy because you say it is so." These quotes are not manufactured by me; they come from the pen of a psychologist whose books have sold in the millions. It is heady stuff, to be sure, but what does it mean? One doesn't need any training in logic to see that his reasons are not reasons at all but only a kind of wishful thinking. It's like saying "I am the most brilliant person in the world because I say I am." It proves nothing.

The next thing to see is that this attitude toward the self flatly contradicts the Christian one. The idea that "your worth is determined by you" is about as far from the gospel message as one could travel. Our Lord's greatest wrath wasn't directed at obvious sinners like Mary Magdalene but at those who were convinced of their own worth. And He never asked His disciples to have self-confidence, only to have faith in Him. There is not the slightest hint in the New Testament that we should have faith in ourselves. As for the proof of our worth, it lies in the fact that God has made us His children and Christ has redeemed us. That, to me, seems a more solid base for our value than the self-asserted kind. I can imagine being admitted into the household of heaven on the grounds that I am a relation, even though a poor one, but I would not want to take my chances on the grounds that I had always practiced self-esteem.

Normal Self-Love: Three Kinds

Am I saying ordinary self-esteem is bad? No. There seems to be a certain level of self-regard that is natural to the numan species. The expression "it's good to be alive" captures it. When we are healthy and hearty and things are going our way, it is perfectly natural to feel good about ourselves. This is nothing other than taking a delight in God's creation, adding our second to, "God saw that it was good." First, then, is a self-love based on our worth as God's handiwork.

In addition, there is a second form of normal self-love: wishing our own happiness. The scriptural command to love our neighbor as ourself seems to assume this. And there is no suggestion anything is wrong with it. Every man wishes the good for himself. That is the way we are built.

To these two kinds of legitimate self-esteem may be added a third: feeling good about ourselves because we are or have been useful, because we somehow fit into a purposeful scheme. The best illustration of this that I know of is the film, *It's a Wonderful Life*. The life of the hero, George Bailey, seems to have come to a dead end, and he is at the point of suicide when an "angel, second class," in the form of a delightful old man, comes to his rescue. I'm sure you know the story. George wishes he had never been born, and the angel temporarily grants the wish. But the world into which George Bailey had never been born is far the worse because of it. It seems there was a special place in the universe that only he could fill. Christianity, of course, says much the same thing. The most downtrodden and powerless man can take heart at the thought that he serves a purpose in God's plan, even if God alone knows what it is.

Notice, however, the difference between these types of self-love and the type based on self-assertion. The first three come under the heading of what might be called "innocent" self-love. It's a thing you can't help: you can't help wishing happiness for yourself, and you can't help feeling good when your life seems purposeful. But the other type is a more arrogant thing. Now, an arrogant person is one who makes unwarrantable claims to dignity, authority, or knowledge. When a psychologist urges you to think "you are worthy because you say it is so," that is an encouragement to arrogance. When the same psychologist says you are to look upon yourself as "the most beautiful, exciting, worthy person ever," that is clearly arrogance. In both cases we would be claiming an authority to bestow on ourselves a status that is not ours to give. It is arrogance and, we might add, not good psychology. It won't wash in most cases, and in any event, it's not what we really need.

Imagine the angel trying to convince the despairing George Bailey that his life matters on the grounds that "you say it's so." Like most of us Mr. Bailey wants something else than his own word for it. Moreover, he doesn't need to hear that he is an intelligent or wonderful person: he needs to see that his life has a purpose.

The trouble with "self-help" self-esteem is that it suggests we are really above the scheme of things. Rather than being a part of creation, the implication is that we are somehow our own creation. "With practice at self-love," as one manual puts it, ". . . you'll believe so much in you that you won't need the love or approval of others to give you value." Now this sounds more like a description of God than of man. God is self-sufficient, but we, despite our worth, are still creatures who do depend on the love of others and, especially, on the love of God.

You see, I trust, that we are no longer in the realm of innocent self-love but in the realm of pride and arrogance. Many of the books on self-esteem start off with something like the innocent version, but then, before you know it, they are sailing off in the direction of self-sufficiency and self-worship—as indeed we all do once we cut our mooring to the virtue of humility.

The Obsessive Concern with Self

The irony is that happiness does not lie in the direction of self-worship. Once we start to concentrate on our dignity as a person or our self-worth, we soon lose the pleasure of innocent self-liking. Cut off from its proper context, concern with self-esteem quickly becomes concern with self-sufficiency, status, power, and the like. This is the pattern of the self-help books, which begin in self-love but always seem to end in self-defense: "You don't need others," "assert yourself," "don't lose out," "don't let them take advantage." One gets the idea that self-esteem needs to be worn like a suit of armor.

Such advice must surely cause us to raise some questions. Why should we be so cautious when surrounded by so many good people like ourselves? And why the obsessive concern with coming out on top that pervades self-help literature and seems to take precedence over self-esteem? There is a contradiction here really. You would expect that if good self-concept were the central thing, you wouldn't have to worry about being a winner or looking out for number one. You would expect that liking yourself would be enough. Clearly, it is not.

Something else is at work, clamoring for attention, spreading its claim wider and wider. Whatever that something is, it is the very antithesis of a workable society where each one submits to a pattern of mutual duty, each one having authority in this matter but not in that, each by turn a leader and then a follower, a teacher and then a student. How wonderful and how rare to find that attitude today. What we glimpse instead is an abrasive collection of selves, each one pressing his claim to the limit.

CHAPTER 4

Wishful Thinking

Do you know the story of *The Little Engine That Could?* I enjoy the part where he repeats over and over "I think I can, I think I can, I think I can," until the refrain has the rhythm of a steam-driven piston. It's a fine story to read to children and also a perfect illustration of positive thinking. It should be tempered, of course, with other kinds of stories so a child will be prepared for those times in life when the tracks ahead are blown up or the bridge is washed out.

While a positive mental attitude can summon strengths and energies we didn't know we had, it can't accomplish miracles. Yet, one of the curious things about a secularized society is this: the less it believes in God, the more it believes in miracles. A paradoxical fact about our supposedly hard-headed nation is that so many grown-ups nourish their minds on the adult equivalent of the *Little Engine* story. The literature of popular psychology is almost exclusively a literature of positive thinking taken to the extreme. Read the most popular psychology titles, and see what miracles are possible. Would you like to cure your cancer? Prevent jet planes from crashing? Fly (without a plane)? Live forever? All these things, you will be told, can be accomplished by mind power.

Positive Thinking or Pretense?

Popular psychology really has little choice but to adopt

this wishful thinking. Its idea about self-esteem is unrealistically based to begin with: the logic of the premise forces the conclusion. Once you elect to believe that you are the pick of the crop simply because you believe it, you are already involved in a fiction. And the initial fraud has to be covered by another and another. Thus, one celebrated psychologist tells us: "You can stand naked in front of a mirror and tell yourself how attractive you are." Yes, you can do that; you can also tell yourself you are rich and brilliant. It may or may not be true. But supposing it is not; what is the point of the pretense?

Please understand that I'm not suggesting we belittle ourselves. Nor do I deny the kernel of truth in positive thinking: when we practice self-confidence we often do appear more attractive to others. If my colleagues would confine themselves to pep talks on this level, I doubt I would object so much. But, of course, it doesn't stop there. The further suggestion is that, since we determine all things for ourselves, we can get along without religion, community, tradition, and family. This isn't merely a suggestion: it is the persistent claim of psychologist after psychologist, book after book.

This is far more harmful stuff than thinking yourself a bit more attractive than you really are. The man who takes the doctrine of autonomy to heart and empties his life of past ties and traditional supports will usually find—perhaps too late—that his inner self won't fill up the hole that is left. The idea that we can love ourselves so much that we won't need the love and help of others is a fiction. None of the statistics suggest it. In fact, they all point the other way: societies that concentrate on the self fall victim to higher rates of loneliness, depression, and suicide than do societies that rely on tradition and community. And do we need statistics to prove what we know deep in our heart?

What about the times when our whole destiny hung upon the health of a sick child? Or the times we've wept through the night, clawing at our pillow out of loneliness? True, some people pass beyond these kinds of vulnerability, but often that is because their personality has withered rather than grown. The man who is autonomous of his family and friends is in the same category as the plant that is autonomous of its soil.

Denying Reality

The denial of our dependence is really a denial of reality. Now the strange thing about the humanistic psychologist, the thing you must grasp before you will understand him, is that this charge doesn't bother him. He very often doesn't give two hoots about reality. He cares much more about *perceptions*. Whether or not those perceptions match reality is not a cause for great concern. This is why human potential psychologists are fond of saying "You make your own reality." You have to understand that in many cases they mean this quite literally, for most of them eventually end up adopting some form of Eastern religion or philosophy. That means, of course, adopting the attitude that matter is an illusion. Once they've settled that in their mind—and the mind, according to Eastern thought, is the only reality—they are free to think as positively as they please. "Mind over matter" is no mere figure of speech for them; it is their ruling belief. It is, of course, the inevitable consequence of basing their psychology on thin air.

The person who starts off with the notion that the self is somehow its own creator will find himself pushed by the logic of that idea further and further from reality until he finally gives up the battle altogether. This is the path followed by the major figures in humanistic psychology: Abraham Maslow, Gardner Murphy, Erich Fromm, Carl Rogers, Michael Murphy (the founder of Esalen), and by popularizers such as Wayne Dyer, Leo Buscaglia, and Will Schutz. To one degree or another, they have all made the journey East.

In Rogers's latest book, *A Way of Being*, there is a chapter entitled "Do we need a reality?" The answer, as you might expect, is no. Rather, says Rogers, there are as many realities as there are people, and what is real for me now is not real for me tomorrow, and so forth. Given these premises, the belief in unlimited human potential is understandable. It is simply a matter of air expanding in a vacuum: there is nothing to prevent it.

No matter how unrealistic these ideas are, they have had practical consequences. Our society is already more than half-convinced that subjective realities are superior to objective ones. Notice the constant chatter about arriving at your own truths or not imposing your values on others, as though truth and value were purely personal constructs and had nothing to do with things outside yourself.

Part of this attitude, I believe, stems from misplaced kindness. Because we are a society that puts a premium on feeling over thought, we yield to temptation and give the subjectivist argument the final say. In that way, no one will get his feelings hurt when a difference of opinion arises. All can be right; no one has to be wrong.

Consequently, we tend to evaluate beliefs by their degree of personal meaning rather than by an objective criterion. One person says, "I believe in Christianity because it has been meaningful for my life" and another says, "Christianity doesn't have any meaning for me. I've found that Eastern philosophy is more meaningful." And, if the first person is a confused Christian, they end up agreeing they are both right because the current wisdom has it that truth is something that makes you feel good.

Faith Founded on Fact

That attitude, however, is the very antithesis of real Christianity, which insists that faith must be anchored in objective fact. The church has always proceeded on the assumption that reality is what we are built for: the more of it we get, the better off we are. The Christian faith is not founded on beautiful thoughts but on decisive historical events that occurred during the time when Augustus and Tiberius ruled Rome. It stands or falls on the reality of those events. Saint Paul's letter to the Corinthians puts the matter starkly: "If Christ has not been raised, then our preaching is in vain and your faith is in vain."

What our Lord came to reveal, moreover, was not a set of inspirational themes, but a transcendent reality, the reality of things as yet unseen but nevertheless fixed and solid. Even when Christians in the past disagreed among themselves, they at least agreed on that. The crucial religious question that cut like a knife through antiquity, through the Middle Ages, and up to the dawn of the twentieth century was "Is it true?" For that question, empires rose and fell, wars were launched, martyrs spilled their blood, and—less dramatically but perhaps more characteristically—feastmakers spilled their wine and danced in the streets through a calendar year illuminated by holidays which were really holy days—holy because they memorialized certain immense facts.

This is a very difficult thing for the modern mind, soaked in psychology, to grasp. It has a different criterion of belief. The question people ask now, whether of a religion or anything else, is "Is it healthy for you?" By which they mean, "Will it contribute to your self-concept?" "Does it make you feel better about yourself?" Not "Is it true?" but "Does it meet my needs?" But let's not allow psychology's success at substituting a therapeutic criterion for a factual one prevent us from calling a spade a spade. It's a question of honesty.

Lewis put the matter well: "If Christianity is untrue, then no honest man will want to believe it, however helpful it might be: if it is true, every honest man will want to believe it, even if it gives him no help at all."[1] This is the reverse of the therapeutic mentality. It shows a mind occupied with something more than need fulfillment. Faith does help. Lewis would have been the first to argue that; but this should not be the standard by which it is judged. The main question to be asked of any faith, be it faith in Christ or faith in psychology, is not "Does it answer needs?" but "Does it answer questions?"

There are many things that will make us feel good about ourselves: a glass of wine, a hot bath, a pleasant daydream. But a philosophy or a faith should not be chosen on the basis of its ability to warm us up. And it certainly should be more than a daydream.

The Mind's First Duty

The mind's first duty, then, is not to prefer pleasant thoughts but to record things as they are. All rational discourse presupposes that we will not go around making up ideas and beliefs to suit our preference. For example, imagine two cars, one moving smoothly through traffic and the other abandoned in a ditch with its engine, doors, and all four tires missing. The second object is still a car, but it is much less a car than the first one. It doesn't correspond as closely to what a car really should be. Next, imagine a collection of car parts—alternators, water pumps, hoses, axles, carburetors, tires—scattered at random over a junk yard. You could say, "That's a car too, if you think about it the right way." But it takes a lot of imagining; in fact you have shifted the emphasis to your own imagination and away from what is really there.

Now this is obvious in regard to cars. But if we take the matter to a different level, it is not quite so obvious even though it is essentially the same problem and even though definitions may be stretched to the breaking point. For example, we now have much disagreement about the definition of *family*. One person might say that a family requires at least one parent and one child. Another might say that a couple without children is a family. Some would even say that homosexual lovers constitute a family.

At some point, however, most of us would draw the line. We have the conviction that some definitions of the family are truer than others. Otherwise we would have to say that words are completely meaningless. Few of us, for instance, would call two strangers sitting together on a bus a family. We still feel that our thought should have some objective basis in reality.

Once that residue of objectivity is lost, we are in for an interminable bout of quarrels and dissension that no amount of sensitivity training can save us from, and which in the end will only be resolved by brute power. If social and moral judgments are nothing but preferences, the preferences of those with the loudest voices and the most push will come to prevail. I chose the family as an example because it happens to be one of those concepts that loud-voiced people are now trying to redefine to suit themselves, and in ways that may do incalculable harm to our children and their children. But, of course, there are innumerable other concepts that people seem bent on moving from the objective side of the ledger to the subjective side: criminal behavior, normal sexuality, marriage, masculinity, and femininity.

Some of the alterations the social sciences are trying to bring about have a tenuous connection with reality. And many of the claims of popular psychology are obviously untrue: that positive thinking cures all problems, that we can be completely autonomous, that we have unlimited potential. These have practically nothing to do with reality. If that's so, then why doesn't everyone see it? The answer is that some people don't want to see it because there is something to be gained by denying the obvious. That something is the free play of the mind: the individual liberty to think whatever we want. It goes along, of course, with the wish to do whatever we want.

Dogmatic Open-mindedness

I said earlier that our culture's subjectivist attitude comes in part from a desire to maintain a climate of good feelings. But there is the more arrogant reason that says, in effect, "My mind is imperial and I will not submit it either to tradition, or to logic, or to the rule of objective evidence." People don't put it that way, of course. They talk instead about the importance of keeping an open mind. There is such a thing, however, as being dogmatically open-minded. We've all met people who seem more interested in the search for truth than in its acquisition. Their central aim and doctrine is to keep their mind free.

The trouble with this attitude is that the mind soon becomes a slave to the self and to the self's desires. A truly free mind has to maintain a certain independence from self, just as a good teacher has to maintain a certain independence from the wishes of his students. We would feel cheated, for instance, if we hired a tutor to help our son with his math deficiency and the tutor played catch with him instead, on the grounds that that is what the boy wanted to do.

It is sometimes difficult for the mind to face realities, especially if they are uncomfortable realities. But that, at least in part, is what a mind is for. G. K. Chesterton relates a friendly luncheon debate with a broadminded acquaintance: "My friend said that he opened his intellect as the sun opens the fans of a palm tree, opening for opening's sake, opening infinitely forever. But I said that I opened my intellect as I opened my mouth, in order to shut it again on something solid."

A lack of solidity is the overriding problem with self-oriented psychology. The set of beliefs that accompany it do not appear to rest on anything firm. Push a bit on the notion that we are wholly good in our nature, and it falls over. Take society away, and you have *Lord of the Flies*. Strip off ritual and tradition, and you find that you are stripping away your skin. Dig around the objective foundations of knowledge, and you may witness your own house collapsing into the pit.

At the end of *The Sun Also Rises*, Hemingway has Jake Barnes reply to his companion's wishful thinking: "Yes, isn't it pretty to think so?" The ideas we have been discussing are sometimes pleasant ideas, but they do not seem to have much warrant in reality. And a denial of real human limitations is not a good basis for a healthy self-respect. The foundation of a true pride, like a true humility, is truth.

I can imagine, however, a voice saying: "You seem to have some problems with these ideas, but I find that they work for me." The only answer to that is to ask, "Do they?" And that will require another chapter.

CHAPTER 5

The Burden of Self

"The trouble with socialism," wrote Oscar Wilde, "is that it takes too many evenings." Wilde was something of a socialist himself, so he was not out of sympathy with its goals. He must have meant it was a tiresome way to spend one's time. There are more pleasant things to do with one's life than to spend it in endless discussions about the ownership of the means of production.

Socialism and its cousin, Marxism, are serious business. If we subscribe to those beliefs, we find that they have a way of taking over our lives. They move right in, set up house, and start rearranging the mental furniture. Before long they are setting the tone for all our thinking. A serious set of beliefs produces, in short, a *characteristic mentality*. For example, we think of the dedicated Marxist as single-minded, intense, pedantic, not much fun to be with. You probably wouldn't invite him over for an evening of card playing and relaxed conversation. This is a stereotype, to be sure, but stereotypes usually have some basis in reality.

The Serious Society

Suppose we ask, then, what is the characteristic mentality produced by a psychological society? The columnist George Will said something that I think hits close to the mark when he wrote about "the curious modern combination of hedonism and earnestness." We are earnest even about our pleasures. *Earnestness* is perhaps too tame a word. *Seriousness* might be more accurate. The hallmark of the psychological society seems to be an unremitting seriousness.

A case in point is provided by psychologist Gordon Allport in his autobiography. When he visited Freud to make the great man's acquaintance, he was ushered into the inner office and then greeted with silence. To fill up the vacuum, Allport told of an episode on the tram car on his way to Freud's office. A small boy with an apparent dirt phobia kept complaining to his mother, "I don't want to sit there. . . . Don't let that dirty man sit beside me." "When I finished my story," Allport recounts, "Freud fixed his kindly, therapeutic eyes upon me and said, 'And was that little boy you?'"

The problem for us is that the serious tone of the therapist's office has crept into all the areas of our lives. Any ordinary remark we make seems to require analysis by our friends. And we, in turn, can hardly give a piece of advice to them without adding, "It will be good therapy for you." In all matters we seem to have adopted an attitude of eternal vigilance: "Will this activity be good for me?" "Will that person encourage my growth?" "Have you hugged your child today?" The spirit of psychology is much like a calculating spirit.

The Self as God

Where does this psychological seriousness come from? Let me propose an answer that may seem strange at first. It comes from the attempt to take the place of God. Let me explain.

I said earlier that concentration on the self often leads to a brash denial of the need for community and tradition. And that, of course, throws people back on their own resources. A similar sort of thing happens with the role God takes in our lives. The self-cultivator doesn't necessarily stop believing in God, but his concept of God will likely change. If we want to get on with our self-actualization, we will probably favor the kind of God who doesn't interfere in the affairs of men: a God who will just let us be ourselves. We will begin to adjust our idea of God to correspond with our ideas about human potential. The more self-reliant we feel ourselves becoming, the less we will feel a need to rely on Him. We will believe we can do for ourselves many of the things that pious people ask God to do.

From here it is just a small step to the belief that the self is a kind of god. Carl Jung believed something of this sort. In his *Answer to Job*, he seems to suggest that God is in many ways inferior to man and that He would like nothing better than to become a man on a permanent basis. One of Erich Fromm's books is entitled *You Shall Be As Gods*. Will Schutz, a popular psychologist, writes, "I am everywhere, I am omniscient, I am God."[1] A participant in an EST seminar will be told, "You are the supreme being."

What are the effects of such a belief?

One of two things seems to happen. A person either loses any sense of responsibility, or one goes the other direction and assumes far more responsibility than is reasonable. In the first case, we have narcissistic and psychopathic individuals or people who are on the way to becoming one or the other. These are people who, of course, cannot see beyond themselves at all. They simply do not care about others. It shouldn't surprise us that the number of narcissists and psychopaths in our society is increasing. It is one of the natural consequences of believing the therapeutic premise that we should never subordinate our needs to someone else's or to some cause or tradition beyond ourselves.

Just as there are always irresponsible people, there are people who are temperamentally inclined to worry about matters beyond their control. If you are of the second type, you will find that just as soon as you have taken responsibility for your self-actualization, you have also taken responsibility for life's failures and deficiencies. In the past, when a religious view prevailed, actualization was thought to be God's business; people were not thought capable of perfecting themselves. Their best bet was to have faith in God. God's grace freely given would do the rest. As for sins and shortcomings, they were not to be condoned, but they were to be expected.

The climate has changed. Nowadays, we feel we all have an inborn capacity for success in life. If we fail, then we're simply not working up to our potential. We should try harder. The psychological society is a society of great expectations. Provided we are self-aware, we should be able to live up to these expectations. And we should be able to do it even without the help of family or community—or God.

This is a difficult business. The type of person who is decent and concerned, and who in the old days would have relied on God to help him carry out his decent intentions, is now thrown back on himself. Each individual must bear the weight of being a god to himself and to others. This isn't always mere arrogance. Our society isn't geared to reminding us of God's presence or power. Consequently, we feel we have no choice but to assume the burden ourselves. Looked at that way, there's a bit of nobility in the endeavor. But it remains a very serious endeavor. Since the self is perceived to be supremely autonomous and supremely capable, we can never relax and simply let God be God.

Oh, I know that psychologists and self-help experts don't say this in so many words. There is a lot of talk about simply accepting yourself as you are. One would think that's a rather easy thing to do. But apparently this is not the case. Self-help books are really workbooks. Most of them contain long lists of exercises for self-improvement. All of them present a model of competence in personal living, work, and childrearing that few people attain. On reading them, we feel we have fallen short of the mark, just as when reading the Gospels we feel we have fallen short of the mark. It's not quite the same mark, of course, and the prescription you get is different. The gospel message is one of having trust in Someone greater than yourself. The self-help message is to shape yourself up. Some psychologists are more explicit about this than others, but this seems to be the underlying current of advice. Here is one example:

> Nonetheless, as soon as we believe it is possible for a man to become God, we can really never rest for long, never say, "O.K., my job is finished, my work is done." We must constantly push ourselves to greater and greater wisdom, greater and greater effectiveness. By this belief we will have trapped ourselves, at least until death, on an effortful treadmill of self-improvement and spiritual growth. God's responsibility must be our own."[2]

The passage is from *The Road Less Traveled* by M. Scott Peck, a psychiatrist. Needless to say, Dr. Peck, along with Dr. Jung and Dr. Fromm, believes it is possible for a man to become God. In one respect I quite agree with him: it is a treadmill.

A Burden Beyond Our Strength

But—and this is the central point—the burden of being a god is a burden to which we simply are not equal. This is the problem, for example, with telling parents to love their children more. No doubt children need more love than they get. The fact remains, however, that many parents are already giving as much love as they have. Children need a lot of love. Indeed, the Christian religion insists that they have an infinite need for love (a point I should like to return to later). But to keep demanding that parents be godlike in supplying love does not usually increase their effectiveness. It only makes them feel guilty.

The point here, however, is not how effective parents can be. Very likely they could be much more effective if the modern world had not stripped them of the props their ancestors were afforded: authority, community, tradition, and spouses. The point is, when you have nothing and no one to rely on but yourself, life becomes very serious indeed. If, in addition, the self is made out by all the experts to be some sort of holy wonder machine, and if you have not yet found the switch, your burden is that much more.

Put it this way. Imagine that the American Medical Association issues a statement on colds, citing research to show that colds are linked to a poor self-concept, lack of will power, and general defects in character. The study claims to show that good-natured, generous, caring people have far fewer colds than people lacking those traits, and it goes on to say that colds can be cured or prevented by a good dose of self-esteem. Having a cold then becomes a more serious matter than it once was. We can't pass it off on wet weather or free-floating germs. We will have to take responsibility for our own colds. In short order, organizations of Snifflers Anonymous will be formed, and children with colds will be sent off to psychiatrists.

Or again, suppose that the surgeon general's office finds that breathing through the nose rather than through the mouth results in increased longevity and thus launches an advertising campaign to make the point. What will happen? In all likelihood, a number of people who never gave breathing a second thought will develop lung ailments and breathing difficulties. Clinics on how to keep your mouth shut will do a thriving business.

The Unhappy Pursuit of Happiness

I hope the point is clear. The serious pursuit of physical health can easily become an unhealthy obsession. In the same way, a man or woman who seriously pursues mental health or fulfillment is traveling the wrong road. The serious pursuit of happiness becomes an unhappy project.

There is one main reason why this is so. Happiness and self-fulfillment belong to a class of things that cannot be pursued directly. They come about as side effects from other pursuits. The more you try to go after them directly, the more they elude you. We are happiest when we are immersed in a game or a hobby or a conversation and have for the moment forgotten about the pursuit of happiness. That is why an emphasis on self-awareness, a common prescription for happiness, is often self-defeating. Happiness comes more frequently when attention is focused outside the self. If we are truly interested in the pursuit of happiness, we would want to be serious about almost anything else—about horse racing, or eating, or love—but not about ourselves.

Another observation. You find very few people who can pursue self-actualization without devaluing other selves. One of the marks of the man who concentrates on himself is a withdrawal of interest in other people and objects. Finally he comes to view outside concerns as interesting only insofar as they serve his own self-realization. They become merely means to an end. Tools. Throw-aways. This kind of attitude, of course, actually tends to subvert one's chances for actualization. The self does not become more interesting as the world becomes less interesting, only more demanding and restless. Before long, the man who started off pursuing self finds it such a burden that he will make any kind of desperate attempt to get rid of it. He turns to drugs or alcohol or to some other anesthetic.

That is the problem set out in bare bones outline. Let me use a cinematic example to give it flesh. *The Mirror Crack'd*, a film based on an Agatha Christie mystery, shows an interesting contrast between two types of people. A Hollywood film crew comes to an English village to make a movie. The Hollywood types are narcissistic in the extreme and yet racked with anxiety and dependent on pills. They have no interest in anything outside themselves, whereas the English characters have an amateur's interest in everything. Miss Marple, for example, is always to be found gardening, or crocheting, or baking bread, or inquiring after neighbors. Her interests lie outside herself, and thus she makes an excellent amateur detective. She can look objectively at a situation because her interests are rooted in objective realities; her curiosity does not end with herself.

Amateur, you may recall, is the French word for "lover." It denotes a fond interest in the world, a loving care for things outside oneself. When we lose our amateur status, we start to lose our ability to care. Something like this seems to have happened to the Hollywood people in this story. On the subject of themselves they are experts. They know every corner of their needs and wants—the result either of years of analysis or simply of living in a psychological society. What they have lost is the amateur's ability to appreciate the rest of life.

There is a further point to be noticed about the movie. The story is set in the 1950s. In some ways that was a short while ago. But in another sense it is centuries distant. Rural England was still a pre-psychological society.[3] So, in fact, were large stretches of rural America. But Hollywood was by that time thoroughly psychologized. So the actors and the villagers are separated not only because they represent two different cultures but also because they live in two different time frames. The English villagers still live in a pre-Freudian world.

A question logically presents itself here: "Are there no actualized people in the world?" The answer is that there are. We all know individuals who strike us as being more alive and more at ease with themselves than the average person. In addition, they seem to have a genuine interest in the world at large. And they often have the ability to make us feel more ourselves. I would merely make the observation that when one encounters the genuine article and not merely a poseur, it's a good bet he didn't get that way by concentrating on the self.

The argument up to this point has been threefold: (1) the attempt to make the self supreme—a replacement for God—puts an enormous burden on us; (2) concentration on the self is self-defeating since it leads not to self-actualization but to self-seriousness; (3) self-preoccupation leads to a withdrawal of interest in the world and in turn makes the self less interesting.

The next step is to ask: "What kind of world are we creating?"

The Modern Cast of Characters

I began this chapter with a discussion of characteristic mentality and suggested that a psychological society creates a climate of unrelenting seriousness. If approached from another direction, the question of characteristic mentality becomes the question of what characters are missing from the story.

I cannot prove statistically what I am about to say; you will have to check it against your own observations. However, my observation is that in the modern theater of life, not only is the set—tradition, ritual, family—discarded but the cast of characters has been narrowed down alarmingly. The present atmosphere does not allow much room for spirited eccentricity, for that larger-than-life character represented in literature by Sir John Falstaff or Samuel Pickwick and in reality by a man like Samuel Johnson—men, in short, who live their lives with outrageous exuberance.

When we think of these characters, we think fondly; they are like overgrown children. It never occurs to them that growing older means growing more serious about oneself. Johnson, even in his later years, delighted in rolling downhill. Pickwick and Falstaff, likewise, spend their days tumbling from one merry episode to the next. What all three have in common is the capacity to give pleasure by their company and their conversation. The reason is their levity. Beneath the surface vanities, they take themselves lightly. Giving pleasure of the kind they give depends on a basic humility, a recognition that they are but men among men, not special selves on the high road to fulfillment.

Now humility does not mean pretending to be less smart or less talented than you really are. Johnson, for example, knew well enough that few men in London could match his intelligence. He was no fool. Yet, on another level he had a fundamental modesty, a belief that all stand equal in the eyes of God, and that in those eyes all of us must at times look foolish. Johnson, in any event, was not above making a fool of himself. He was glad for any occasion of foolishness and created them when none came to hand. He was, wrote a close friend, "incomparable at buffoonery."

It is hard for lightheartedness to hold the stage, though, once we learn how very seriously we ought to take ourselves. And this is what psychology has taught us. We hear a lot these days, for example, about the dignity of the person. This is a good emphasis if it means that no one ought to exploit or abuse anyone else. But if it means we are to perceive ourselves as solemn godlings and centers of wholeness, the idea can do much harm.

One casualty of our overseriousness may be our sense of humor. And that is because all humor involves a loss of dignity. The man who makes faces to amuse a baby gives up his dignity; so does the man who roars with laughter. The essential condition for having fun is to forget your dignity, that is, to forget yourself. We recognize this truth, for example, when we say, "I was beside myself with laughter." We have to get outside ourselves to enjoy ourselves. Otherwise, we won't have any perspective; we won't see the joke. But an excess of self-preoccupation robs us of all perspective: enter self-seriousness, exit humor.

Exit humor, exit sanity. We sometimes speak of people as having a "saving grace," some quality that keeps them from meanness or dullness, and a sense of humor is certainly one of those saving graces. Among other things, humor helps us save our sanity. This seems true, for example, of Johnson, who was naturally disposed to melancholy and suffered from poverty, grave physical ailments, and a singular physical ugliness as well. Indeed, he feared at some points that he would lose his mind. The remedy, he realized, was not to court self-awareness. The cure consisted rather in getting away from himself. No one can say what would have been the result had psychotherapy been available in those days. But we do know that therapy encourages self-analysis. Perhaps Johnson was fortunate that it was not available.

That Johnson was able to get outside himself we know from the genial legacy of his antics. There is the picture of Johnson gathering up his brown coattails like a pouch and hopping his bulky frame across the room to amuse his guests with an imitation of a kangaroo. And there is Johnson in the London streets bursting "into such a fit of laughter, that he appeared to be almost in a convulsion; and, in order to support himself, laid hold of one of the posts . . . and sent forth peals so loud, that in the silence of the night his voice seemed to resound from Temple-bar to Fleet-ditch."[4]

If we are to obtain wholeness, then, we ought to employ the right strategy. People are most themselves when they get outside themselves.

Self-absorption and Sanity

Extreme forms of mental illness are always extreme cases of self-absorption. Ibsen described a lunatic asylum as a place in which "each shuts himself in a cask of self, the cask stopped with a bung of self, and seasoned in a well of self."[5] People suffering from paranoia, for example, are unable to let their attention wander. You won't find them absent-mindedly gazing at flowers. If they are looking at flowers, they are looking for the seed of a conspiracy directed at them.

The distinctive quality, the thing that literally sets paranoid people apart, is hyper-self-consciousness. And the thing they prize most about themselves is autonomy. Their constant fear is that someone else is interfering with their will or trying to direct their lives. For this type of person, self-abandonment is the worst fate. Rather than have that happen, they draw deeper into themselves, cutting the cords of sociability as they go.

In an excellent study of this sickness, David Shapiro observes: "Paranoid people rarely laugh. They may act as if they are laughing, but they do not laugh genuinely; that is, they do not feel amused." Why not? Because "laughing always involves a certain degree of abandonment." Again: "Not only the range of affects but also the range of interests contracts and narrows in these people. Playfulness disappears and playful interests are usually absent."[6]

(I'm not suggesting that people who suffer from mental illnesses of this sort are self-absorbed willfully. They simply are unable to break out of their mental prisons.)

Now a step further. You may wonder at this point about another type of mental illness: depression. Depressed people do not seem to worry about their autonomy. They don't seem to care about anything for that matter. If you have ever been depressed, you know the feeling. Life seems worthless, without hope. The self, too, seems worthless and empty. The depressed person would like nothing better than to get outside himself, but he can't. The world seems as hopeless as the self. The depressed person knows that he needs to be rescued, but he doesn't believe in the possibility of rescue. He can't abandon himself because he fears there is nothing or no one to rely on.

Unlike the one who is paranoid, the depressed person has no illusions about autonomy. Yet the basic similarity, the thing you notice in both cases, is the centrality of self. The paranoid person believes the self is all there is and tries desperately to control it. The depressed person fears the self is all there is and is in despair.

If I were depressed, the last thing I would want to hear is, "At least you've got yourself." The depressed person has already tried self-reliance, and when the real test came, it failed. If the self is all he has to live for, he'd rather die. Of all people, he is in the best position to appreciate George MacDonald's observation: "The one principle of hell is—'I am my own.'"

Objections to the Self-image Argument

Some will object to this interpretation and say that victims of depression never had a sense of self-worth to begin with. They need, it will be said, to learn their own value. Then they won't come apart the next time a job falls through or a lover walks out on them. But consider these objections to that view:

(1) Suppose it is true that the depressed person lacks a good self-image. Where is that good image to come from now? From inside? But the person is sunk in despair. From us? But we can't replace the lost job or the lost lover. Telling him he needs a good image of himself is like telling a man with eye problems that he needs better vision. It's not very helpful.

(2) A related problem is that psychologists have contradictory things to say about the origin of self-image. On the one hand, child psychologists suggest that self-image is our parents' responsibility. If they were good parents and loved us, then we will have good self-concepts. If they were bad parents, then we will have bad self-concepts. This really amounts to saying it's a matter of luck. Good self-image is good luck, and bad self-image is bad luck. On the other hand, adult psychologists seem to say that we can change our luck anytime we wish. We can rise above fate and circumstances and somehow establish our self-image independent of the vagaries of fortune. But just how does one do that?

(3) Implicit in the self-image argument is the notion that people with a good self-image don't suffer from serious depression. No they don't . . . as long as life is going well for them, just as a thief is an honest man when he's not stealing. Again, it's a question of which comes first: our good luck or

our good self-image? Take away the good luck, and the self-image begins to crumble. Very few people stand up well in the face of sudden and serious illness, the loss of a job, or the end of a marriage or love affair. Do we then say to them that their self-concept must not have been very good to start with?

(4) The self-image argument further suggests that autonomous, self-validating people don't suffer from depression. No they don't, not if they have made themselves so uncaring that the loss of another leaves them unaffected. Psychopaths don't suffer from depression. In the long run, the answer to the proponents of autonomy is a question: "What are you asking us to do? Should we so armor ourselves with self-sufficiency that we become invulnerable not only to being hurt but to ever getting close enough to be hurt?"

(5) The philosophy of self-esteem is everywhere. One would think that by now it would have had time to take effect. Yet depression is rampant. So is suicide. Adolescent suicide is up almost 300 percent over the last twenty-five years. Suicide among children—at one time a rare phenomenon—is on the rise. The philosophy of self-esteem doesn't cause these problems, but it doesn't seem to prevent them either. "I arm you with the sword of self-esteem," says the psychological society to its children. "It will serve you well in battle." But it is not a good weapon, and our enemies are not so easily slain. The power of the opposition has been sadly underestimated, and our own powers greatly exaggerated.

When All Else Fails

These are unpleasant words, especially if your faith is rooted in psychology and its main champion, the self. The self fails, and it fails patently, time after time. Others fail us as well. The plain truth is, when these fail, psychology has nothing left to offer. If you are looking for something that doesn't fail, the psychological society is not the place to look.

The psychological perspective, by the way, is not a new one. In the fifth century a British monk named Pelagius proposed the heretical belief that people are responsible for their own salvation. An austere and zealous man, he had little sympathy with human failings. "Try harder," he said in effect; "no slouching; learn self-discipline; pull yourself up by your boot straps; be master of your fate; trust yourself, and stop crying to God."

To which Christians say, as did Falstaff defending his motley crew of soldiers before the prince, "Tush man, mortal men, mortal men." Mortal men: that is, frail, sometimes cowards, often foolish. Perhaps this does not say as much for human dignity as we would like. But there it is. And it speaks for all the failed and frustrated of this world, not just the few who have made it.

It happens also to be a more realistic approach to contentment. Christianity says you can't depend on yourself and you can't ultimately depend on others either. Salvation is basically God's work. Happiness lies in recognizing that fact. When the self fails and when all else fails in addition, all is not necessarily lost.

Carefree or Careful?

The difference between the self as savior and God as savior is the difference between care and carelessness, that is, between one who is full of care and one who is carefree. One difference between a healthy person and a neurotic one is a certain air of carelessness in the healthy one. People who are content aren't constantly worrying about their health.

They don't do things for "good therapy" but simply because they enjoy doing them. They aren't paying constant attention to their inner processes.

We can't afford to be carefree, however, if we believe that at every moment "it's all up to me." As soon as you make the self its own savior, you are on that "effortful treadmill" that Dr. Peck described so well. You must walk carefully from that moment on.

That leads to one last point. When we get careless we tend to lose things: keys, gloves, glasses. That is the irritating aspect of it. How pleasant, though, when we find we have lost ourselves—in conversation, in reverie, in work, or in play. The best times are those high moments of self-loss, moments when, immersed in talk or lost in laughter, we are more ourselves than ever. To be ready for such moments, the best preparation is to travel lightly.

Chesterton suggested of Pickwick that he was sustained by the hint "which tells him in the darkest hour that he is doomed to live happily ever afterward." Chesterton himself reminds us of Pickwick: a fat jovial man of irrepressible good spirits. And in *The Man Who Was Thursday*, Chesterton's fantastical mystery story, we come face to face with the most buoyant character of all—Sunday, the colossal president of the Anarchist Club, a man so huge you think he would crack the sidewalks when he walks. Yet Sunday bounces off the street like an Indian rubber ball and eludes his captors at the last by sailing aloft in a balloon. Sunday, of course, turns out to be. . . . Well, it would spoil the story to tell you in advance.

The point I have been at pains to make is that buoyancy is hard to come by in a psychological society. We are too weighted down by our own gravity, too freighted with self-calculation. Psychological seriousness even infects our humor. We have intelligent humorists: men like Woody Allen, Jules Feiffer, Gary Trudeau. But much of their humor is psychiatric in origin. It is a self-conscious type of humor, not a self-forgetful kind. It is hard to imagine Woody Allen throwing his head back with Dr. Johnson and roaring with laughter.

And we do need to laugh—particularly at the state we have got ourselves in by taking psychology and ourselves so very seriously. There must be better ways to spend our time. If Oscar Wilde could say, "The trouble with socialism is that it takes too many evenings," perhaps we can wonder if the same is not true of psychology: that it takes up too many evenings . . . and too many afternoons as well.

CHAPTER 6

Sin and Self-acceptance

Christianity doesn't make sense without sin. If we are not sinners, turned away from God, then there was no reason for God to become a man, and no reason for Him to die. Our slavery to sin is the thing that Christ came to free us from. That is the most fundamental Christian belief. It follows that if you have no consciousness of sin, you simply won't be able to see the point of Christianity. We can put the matter more strongly and say that once you grant the notion that people are sinless, you must admit that Christianity is all wrong.

Now it is possible to create a climate in which people have very little sense of sin and, therefore, little chance of comprehending what Christianity is all about. We know it is possible because that is the climate that exists today. The fact is, psychology has been enormously successful in its program to get people to accept themselves—or at least to accept the idea that they ought to accept themselves. Even when people do not, in fact, feel good about themselves, they have the belief they ought to feel good. Even when they feel guilty, they are convinced it is only neurotic guilt: not a matter for expiation but for explanation.

Changing Beliefs Instead of Behavior

Besides creating in us the idea that we should feel good about ourselves, psychology leads us to place a high premium on integration and harmony of personality. The problem here is that for those who still believe in sin, beliefs and actions are often out of harmony. "For I do not do the good I want," wrote Saint Paul, "but the evil I do not want is what I do."

One way to handle this discrepancy between our beliefs and our sinful inclinations is to repent, pray for grace and forgiveness, and struggle on in the belief that God will forge a greater harmony for us out of our battle with sin. That is the Christian approach. The new psychological idea seems to be that we should have harmony at any price. If our actions aren't in line with our beliefs, then we ought to change the beliefs (beliefs being considerably easier to change than behavior).

This, upon examination, is what a lot of the talk about "improving your self-concept" amounts to. It means that if your self-concept won't let you feel good about having casual sex, and yet you still want casual sex, then you ought to adjust your self-concept accordingly. The alternative is feeling bad about yourself, and that seems an almost unacceptable alternative these days. All of this involves a lot of shuffling and wriggling and devious logic. It means convincing ourselves that what we want to do isn't so bad after all. It's basically dishonest, of course. There was something more creditable about the person who could say, "This is wrong, but I just can't help myself," or "This is wrong, but I don't care anymore. I must have it."

You might think, then, that an appeal to honesty would be the appeal of last resort in our society. But that is not the case. Curiously enough, a lot of our moral jiggery pokery *is* justified in the name of honesty. The psychological creed says that we ought to be proud of ourselves and our lifestyles, that we should not hide what we are.

There is a widely used training film for counselors that

shows a divorced woman who is troubled with the problem of whether or not to let her daughter know she sleeps with the men she dates. On the one hand, she wants to be honest with her daughter; on the other hand, she feels ashamed. At one point she very frankly tells the therapist, "I want to have you help me get rid of my guilt." And that, of course, is what he does. Afterwards, the therapist observes of this episode that the woman moved "from not accepting herself to accepting herself."

This particular therapist, who is by the way quite famous, has always marveled in his books at how completely people can come to accept themselves. But it is small wonder, given the sort of encouragement they receive. Part of the trick is to reinforce the obviously noble part of the patient's conflict—in this case the mother's desire to maintain an open relationship with her child. In the psychological society, honesty is allowed to cover a multitude of sins. Unfortunately, it is also allowed to cover the natural sense of shame, which is one of the keepers of our goodness. It is none of our business here to pass sentence on a woman who is caught in the coils of a difficult and all too common predicament; what needs to be seen, rather, is that the counseling process she is subjected to is a formula for insuring that consciousness of sin is diminished. We must esteem honesty, but a truly honest person will want to know what kind of honesty it is that keeps arriving at the conclusion that nothing really wrong has been done.

Becoming Worse through Self-acceptance

It can be objected here that self-acceptance has many positive benefits. True enough. Some people become better people through self-acceptance: they learn to accept their limitations and shortcomings, and consequently they can accept the limitations of others. They stop trying to be perfectionists and learn to be thankful for the gifts they do have. But it is equally true that others become worse through self-acceptance.

Picture a fairly decent man who tries to suppress his tendency to anger, makes sacrifices for the sake of others, tries to keep his sexual instincts in line, tries hard, in other words, to be good. Then he comes across a book or two that tell him he's already good. He's told that his impulses can be trusted, that he shouldn't be afraid to be himself, that there's no reason to be ashamed of his anger or sexual instincts, because these, after all, are human things. A lion, he might be told, isn't ashamed of doing the things lions do, so why should a man be ashamed of doing the things that come naturally to him? Since our man has been rather a good person, none of this will be hard to believe. He may even be inspired by the appeals to personal growth and courage that characterize these books. His self-acceptance will be made to look like an act of bold virtue. What he has latched onto, in fact, is a naturalistic philosophy that fails to notice that the nature of human beings is quite different from the nature of other animals. There are instinctual limits that control an animal's behavior, but when a man begins to act on instinct alone, there is quite literally nothing that he may not do.

Our man starts to look at things in a new light. Gradually his attitude alters. He begins to think he has been denying himself his natural rights and needs. He had always had an inclination to try such-and-so, but always in the past he had kept that inclination bridled. Soon he looks upon it not as a temptation but as an opportunity for growth. The question for him is no longer "Is it right or wrong?" but "Is it a growthful experience?" or some such formula. A "growthful experience," of course, is like a "learning experience"—everything seems to qualify. Before long, he will be doing things he once would have thought abominations. He will lose altogether his ability to see these things for what they are. Instead of becoming more self-aware, he will blunt his power to make moral distinctions.

When Sin Becomes Second Nature

The fact that we can and do get used to things to the point where they become second nature, says nothing for their rightness or wrongness. Some people grow accustomed to being slaves, others to being prostitutes. "Do not," wrote Chesterton, "be proud of the fact that your grandmother was shocked at something which you are accustomed to seeing or hearing without being shocked. . . . It may mean that your grandmother was an extremely lively and vital animal, and that you are a paralytic." This is the problem with the habit of ready self-acceptance. Like other habits, it sometimes puts a stop to thought and paralyzes our ability to make appropriate responses.

This, of course, is what Christianity has always said about habits of sin. Part of the problem with seeing our own sinfulness is that the more we sin, the more our ability to see sin is clouded. When a man is drunk, drunkenness does not seem like such a bad thing unless he is drunk to the point of throwing up. At the height of an illicit sexual encounter, the sex seems like rather a good thing. It is only afterwards that there are second thoughts. But if we make illicit sex our habitual mode, even those afterthoughts will disappear. Give enough practice to your inclination to cheat and double-deal, and before long you'll stop thinking of it as fraud and call it good business sense.

To be objective about our own sins is very difficult and more so if we've developed a habit of ready self-acceptance. We are too close to them, too cozy and comfortable. The psychological view can be more readily tested with regard to other people. Now it is very easy to speculate how pleasant the world would be if people could learn to accept themselves. But think what this would mean. Think, for instance, of the people who make life difficult for you or for someone you care about. You have seen the cruelty in their character, the self-centeredness, the absence of fair play, the ruthless manipulation of others. Would you really have them accept themselves as they are? Wouldn't that be adding insult to injury? And isn't it a fact that often this sort of person does accept himself and even glories in his faults? "Yes, I'm selfish. What of it? Nobody's going to take advantage of me," or "Sure I'll lie if I have to: that's the way the world works." We know people like that. We know others who brag about how many women they've seduced. Wouldn't you like to see such people change before accepting themselves—not simply for the sake of those around them but for their own sakes? Before it's too late?

A Grumbler or a Grumble?

I say "before it's too late," because repeated sin like repeated blisters has a way of hardening into something calloused and insensitive. It is this hardening process, not the occasional lapse, that the Christian churches have always warned against most vigorously. The slow accumulation of petty vindictiveness, quarrelsomeness, sulkiness, and similar habits will in the long run prove more dangerous to your soul than the glaring misdeed, acknowledged and repented. Lewis, in *The Great Divorce*, describes a woman whose life is one of constant grumbling, and he observes that the main question to ask is whether she is "a grumbler, or only a grumble." One can begin with a grumbling mood, and yet remain distinct from it, still able to criticize and resist it. "But there may come a day when you can do that no longer. Then there will be no *you* left to criticize the mood, nor even to enjoy it, but just the grumble itself going on forever like a machine." I am afraid we have all met people like this, caught up in the vise grip of some mood or obsession to the point where there seems to be nothing human left, only the mood itself existing as a hard and empty casing.

Christianity speaks of this as slavery to sin. The worst form, of course, is when you arrive at a state where the sin has taken over so completely that you do not even realize your slavery. But you can also be well aware of your slavery and still be unable to do much about it. We speak for instance of people who are "consumed" with lust or rage, or of people who are in the "grip" of envy. There is a good deal of psychological truth in these well-worn phrases. The word *consumed*, for instance, suggests quite correctly that the personality is being eaten up or burned away. When something like this happens to us, we can actually feel the destruction of our personality. We know that if we continue in it there will be nothing left of us; yet we feel almost helpless to control these passions. We know, for example, that the desire for revenge can so warp and twist a man that even while he is perishing from it, losing his friends and perhaps his sanity, he will cling to the revenge, nourish it, and even prefer it to any good thing he might enjoy.

We shouldn't congratulate ourselves if we have escaped these extreme forms of bondage. There are other, more widespread forms. Any sinful habit that we can't break makes us slaves to sin. We admit as much any time we advise others against getting started on bad habits that have mastered us. That is why parents sometimes find themselves in the awkward position of telling a child not to do things that they themselves do. It is hard for the child to understand why, if a certain behavior is so bad, you don't stop behaving that way yourself. He doesn't yet know about these kinds of slavery, nor how hard it is to stop a bad habit. It would be better for you to set a good example for him, but if you can't do that, the next best thing is to swallow your pride and tell him that there are standards worth living up to, even though you don't always live up to them. You may have lost much of your freedom to live up to them, but you hope that he will not.

Forging Chains

An irony here is that people who think there is nothing funny about compulsive gambling or drinking or promiscuity will ridicule those who try to set down the necessary first steps for avoiding such habituations. The catechism I learned as a boy states simply: "Little boys and girls are not usually in danger of committing mortal sins. But they can commit little sins. And if they commit venial sins on purpose when they are small and do not try to avoid them, they will commit big sins when they grow up." That sort of reasoning is considered a joking matter today, but it happens to be very proper psychology. The battle is won or lost here: over the little habits, over the initial temptations. One thing does lead to another, either to a hardening into virtue or into vice. It has to do with forging chains, as Marley's ghost found out too late.

I present these thoughts not as theological speculation but as psychological fact. Once you remove the label "slavery to sin," most people will be willing to admit the phenomenon.

Most people can understand easily enough the concept of being a slave to drugs or drink or cigarettes or even chocolate. In some cases, as we know, it can amount to a very complete slavery. A person loses his freedom in the matter. He cannot stop. He has lost control. We know also that some people become slaves to sex. In fact, it is an idea that pornographers play on with the use of terms like *love slave*. Then there is the obvious irony that the more liberated society becomes in regard to sex, the more obsessed it becomes with sexual bondage.

Sin and Sickness

There is ample evidence that the phenomenon Christians call "slavery to sin" does, in fact, exist. You may, as is the modern habit, call it what you like, but there are reasons not to remove the label. The words *sin, repentance,* and *forgiveness* all imply freedom and responsibility. When you take away those labels, you very often take away freedom and responsibility as well. Now this is what has happened by and large. We have taken the phenomenon of slavery to sin and renamed it "sickness." Christians can go along part way with this idea, because they believe that one form of sin—original sin—is, in effect, a genetic disorder. But when we come down to particular sins, the Christian will not be so hasty about transforming them into medical matters.

In the first place, the parallel between sin and sickness is not a good one. Sin is often seen as an exciting and pleasurable possibility; sickness is not. Men do not pursue arthritis the way they pursue adultery. In the second place, it is a poor compliment to the species: it robs us of the real dignity we have, which is the freedom of choosing the good. The reverse side of the coin stamped "Smith's sin is only a sickness" is "Smith's virtue is vitamin based." It is a way of reducing a human being to the level of a walking chemistry shop. Often it is a disposition to be generous and kind that makes us excuse other people's faults as sicknesses, but how much of a kindness is it? Is that the way we would like others to think of our own misdeeds? Do we want to be patted on the head like children, while some grownup makes excuses for us: "Poor Billy, he can't help himself," or worse, "Poor Billy, he was born with an endorphin deficiency."

Taking People Seriously

The reason Christianity takes sin seriously is that it takes people seriously. It won't let us off with childish excuses for our behavior, because our behavior is held to count most highly. When Christianity talks about the dignity of the person, it gives that phrase an extraordinarily high meaning against which the world's casual use of the phrase is child's talk.

Christianity is a high calling. One of the obstacles to seeing this is our distorted view of who God is. Some of us have succumbed to the idea that if He exists at all, He must be made in the image and likeness of our more understanding and good-natured therapists. This, of course, reduces us to the image and likeness of clients and hospital patients. It is only as we begin again to realize the utter purity and holiness of God that we begin to appreciate that He simply cannot wink at sin like some friar out of the *Canterbury Tales*. Selling sin short is only the reverse side of selling God short. Better here to think of spired kingdoms and awesome magic than to get our picture of God confused with a job description for a professional helper.

If we are God's children or even only His servants, then what we do is, to borrow a phrase from Thomas Howard's *Chance or the Dance*, "wildly charged with significance." If we are called to participate in God's creation, then it can be no small matter whether we do our part well or badly. God does not, if Scripture is any indication, look upon our behavior as a species of interesting natural phenomenon. On the contrary, there is a distinct impression that He looks upon us the way a king regards a knight who is sent on an important mission or as a father looks upon a son for whom he has high hopes.

Half of popular psychology is devoted to praising human dignity and the other half to excusing us from responsibility. But what kind of dignity is that? It's no good to tell a man he's fully human in one breath, and then with the next suggest he's no more accountable than a vegetable. These contradictions in theory eventually do show up in practice. The current disarray of our criminal justice system is one example: it has relied far too much on psychological concepts of guilt and responsibility—concepts that have brought the system almost to a dead end. The reluctance to convict, the backlog of court cases, and the increase in criminal behavior are due at least in part to the new notion that right and wrong are to be measured by psychological rather than legal and moral criteria, and to the equally dubious notion that judges and juries should play the role of therapists. The Hinckley case is only the most conspicuous example of the problem.

Why then are we so quick to accept every new psychological pronouncement? Once again I return to the thesis that psychology derives much of its acceptability from its resemblance to Christianity. Because it has transferred the language of Christianity to its own uses, it is able to play on Christian sentiments to an extraordinary degree. I think for many of us psychology seems to provide a way of getting Christianity "on the cheap."

For instance, one of the themes that runs through both Christianity and psychology is the idea that we shouldn't make judgments about one another. Our Lord said "judge not," and if nothing else, the psychological society does seem faithful to that. This nonjudgmental attitude, which gives psychology a Christian aura, perhaps accounts for the present inclination to drop the whole matter of sin. Too much talk of sin doesn't seem to square with our duty to judge not.

What "Judge Not" Really Means

But "judge not" means we are not to judge a man's inner state. It does not mean we are not to judge his acts. Christ did not say to the woman caught in adultery, "That's O.K. You really haven't done anything wrong." He told her to "sin no more." This distinction tends to get lost, however, in our therapeutic society. Instead of maintaining the attitude "hate the sin and love the sinner," we are no longer sure if we have any right to hate the sin or even to call it that. In fact, the Christian injunctions have been nearly reversed. We now refrain from judging a person's acts but spend all sorts of energy trying to judge his moods and motivations, which is properly God's function, not ours. Perhaps one of the reasons we are not to judge subjective states is that we are simply not equipped to do so. The matter is too complicated for us.

A sense once prevailed that it was ultimately God's business, not ours, to plumb a person's inner labyrinth. By and large, we are capable of judging whether Tommy Thompson stole the money out of the cash drawer, and we may go a bit further and take into account Mr. Thompson's frustration over being unemployed and his lack of opportunity. For those reasons perhaps we will deal more leniently with him. But how much further should we go? Should we go into his childhood upbringing? Into the television shows he watches? Into his rich (or deprived) fantasy life? Into the symbolic meaning of cash drawers in his life? There is a point, as Chesterton noted, where you start trying "to calculate the incalculable." At that point, even our calculations for good become not calculations but incantations and mumbo jumbo. We have gone beyond our scope.

Getting on Board a Sinking Ship

Christians, as I suggested earlier, sometimes tend to act on psychological theories long before the psychologists are done thinking about them. Other times, unfortunately, they can be noticed getting on board ship at the precise moment when psychologists are ready to abandon it. Some of the most distinguished psychologists—Coles, Menninger, Bettleheim, Mowrer, Campbell, and Gaylin—have worked in recent years to reinstate concepts of sin and guilt. Others have come to see that self-esteem or the lack of it is too shallow a concept to be of much help in analyzing the human predicament.

Meanwhile, while all this has been going on, one of the leading Christian evangelists has taken it into his head that the cause of sin is "negative self-image," and that sin itself must now be redefined as "any act or thought that robs myself or another human being of his or her self-esteem." The same man now defines being born again to mean that "we must be changed from a negative to a positive self-image."

A similar tendency can be seen in religious education textbooks now used in liberal Catholic and Protestant churches. One can read these and come away with the impression that the beginning and end of Christianity is to love oneself. Sin is rarely mentioned, and when it is, it is pictured more often than not as an impediment to personal growth—something that gets in the way of self-actualization. The texts to which we entrust the Christian education of our young are often barely distinguishable from texts for a psychology class.

The promoters of these programs claim, of course, that the psychology is in line with Scripture: that God's creation is good, that He does not make junk, and so forth. It is, of course, a *selective* reading of Scripture. Genesis does not record any evidence of God's standing back after the Fall and observing that *it* also was good.

In any event, the actual effect of these programs is what one might expect. They act to diminish the consciousness of sin so that even in the Catholic church, which once had a sort of notoriety for cultivating guilt, many children cannot see the point of penance. And this is not because they prefer the Protestant idea of confessing sins straight to God, but because they know of no sins to confess. The only gospel they know is the gospel of O.K.-ness.

I am not sure why Catholics are particularly susceptible to psychologism in this respect. Perhaps they chafed too long under the charge of medievalism and overcompensate now with "relevance." Or perhaps Catholic Christians, who have always been more interested in what might be called the psychology of the soul, are therefore disposed to psychological approaches.

At any rate children in catechism classes nowadays are taught very little about personal sin and individual conscience and a great deal about collective guilt and social conscience. The great sins, the ones we ought to be concerned about, are the sins of society. That is the new emphasis.

Personal Sins

Now there is, without doubt, a place for exposing society's sins. Perhaps they were not stressed sufficiently in the recent past. But Christian educators who emphasize collective sin at the cost of teaching about personal sin are certainly doing a disservice to their charges. Do they suppose that when we are summoned to the judgment place, God will quiz us only on our attitudes about world peace and hunger? That will be an easy exam. How many of us are for hunger or against peace? It's no skin off our noses to wish sincerely for social justice and an end to suffering.

I am afraid, alas, that the questions will be much more personal and disturbing than that. They will have to do with that lonely girl you took advantage of and have now forgotten, or with a sick or imprisoned relative you studiously avoided (perhaps because you were too busy marching for peace), or with your complete cowardice that time you failed to defend an innocent reputation. We shall find then that our private lives and our personal sins are taken with quite a bit more seriousness in heaven than our position on global issues.

I imagine when that time comes we will see things for what they are and what they were. The therapeutic nonsense and easy outs with which we now comfort ourselves will melt away, and our true calling will be unmistakably vivid, just as we always should have seen it had our consciousness been truly raised. It will do no good then to plead that we were only following the best psychological advice available. That was never the advice we were mainly intended to follow. Our best hope then will be the knowledge that the Son of Man came to save sinners and that God's mercy is as great as His justice.

CHAPTER 7

On Being Born Again

The goals of psychology may be roughly summarized under headings such as "adjustment," "coping," "harmony," "fulfillment," "self-confidence," "improved relationships," and so on. These are worthy goals: good harbor for Christian and non-Christian alike. But they should never be confused with the Christian program for mankind—although regrettably they often are. The Christian idea is quite different. It has to do not with an adjustment but with a transformation; not with getting a tune-up but with getting a new engine. Christianity says you have to be born again. That is the long and the short of it. Get fulfillment and wholeness and harmony if you can, but whether you succeed or not you will still need to be born again.

Evidence from Elsewhere

If Christians were the only ones to say this, we would have the problem of "Christianity says this, and psychology says that, and who are you to believe?" So let us look elsewhere for corroboration. If the things Christianity says about human nature are true, we should expect to find supporting evidence for it among people who are not Christian.

The fact is, Christians are not the only ones who say we need to be born again. Most primitive societies believe the same. Their rituals attest to it. We see it in the things they take most seriously, the things they ring with ceremony and spend weeks and months preparing for. Being born once—natural birth—apparently is not enough for them, for their rites of initiation are full of actions and gestures that symbolize rebirth.

Crocodiles, Sweathouses, and Ram Skins

The most common initiation ritual is running the gauntlet: a candidate runs through a tunnel formed by two parallel lines of men who hit him with switches as he goes. If you concentrate on the blood and bruises and "primitiveness" of this ceremony, you will have missed the main point: birth is a traumatic and bloody business. You can't expect a rebirth to be a tame affair like being fitted for a new suit.

Among some tribes in New Guinea, initiation consists of crawling into the open mouth of a crocodile and out the other end. I hasten to add that it is a dead crocodile, and its tail has been cut off. But enough blood and entrails are left inside to ensure that the youngster will know he has taken an extraordinary passage. In the Pacific Northwest, Indian boys must go into a sweathouse as part of the ceremony and sweat themselves down until they are supple enough to squeeze outside through a small hole in the wall. Other tribes in other parts of the world have initiatory huts set off in the bush or jungle where the initiates are confined for weeks or months as in a womb. I think the symbolism is clear.

Now all of this may seem a far cry from the Christian practice of baptism, but the same instinct is there. And this goes right down the line, even to the conviction that to have real life in you, you have to first die to yourself. This is why some peoples bury their candidates for adulthood in shallow graves covered with leaves. And this is why the Bantu have a ceremony called "being born again" in which a boy, prior to circumcision, is wrapped by his father in the stomach membrane of a ram and remains there for three days. Mircea Eliade, the noted religious historian, points out, "The same people bury their dead in ramskins and in the fetal position."[1]

Three days. That's an interesting coincidence, of course, and there are different ways to respond to it. You can say this proves only that Christianity is just another piece of mythology like the rest. But then you are faced with the fact that there exists a surprising amount of this mythology, and all of it points in the same direction. Something that represents a nearly universal impulse should not be put lightly aside. It demands to be explained, not ignored.

Part of the problem here is that we have taken some recent developments in "advanced" societies and assumed them to be the norm. It might be helpful for us to stand back occasionally from the psychological society and think how we must look to the Bantu. When it comes to rituals of transformation, it might be observed by a neutral party that three days in a ramskin is not nearly as bad as seven years in a psychiatrist's office, and far less costly. And, as Huckleberry Finn says, "The wages is just the same." Or better. Friends of mine, missionaries who have lived among the Bantu and other surrounding tribes, tell me that the Bantus are refreshingly free of the neuroses that plague Americans and profit psychologists.

Primitive Wisdom

So it is not just Christians who want to be born again. Whenever we find people who have not yet come under the influence of scholars or advertisers, we find them expressing in one way or another this idea of a second birth.

Nicodemus, who like all the Pharisees was a scholarly man, had a great deal of trouble with the idea: "How can a man be born when he is old? Can he enter a second time into his mother's womb and be born?" The answer of primitive man to that question is surprisingly like the answer of primitive Christianity. Impossible and preposterous as it may sound, it is a thing that ought to be done, if only symbolically.

I don't wish to be misconstrued, however, as saying that Christianity is nothing new, only a variation of an old theme. It represents something radically new in the universe: a revolution, in fact. People could figure out for themselves that something was wrong with human nature, something so twisted that it called for a new birth; but they could never have guessed the whole story or how the thing really was to be done. When Christianity appeared, it came with the message that the transformation people had been yearning for since antiquity could actually be accomplished, not just in symbol but in reality.

My point is that what Christianity brought to the world may have been supernatural, but it was not unnatural. What it offered man was the completion of his nature, not something foreign to it. And almost everywhere where they were given the choice, pagan and primitive people adopted the new Christianity in place of their old beliefs because it gave them, and gave them in detail, the things their nature told them ought to be there. If, by contrast, many scholarly people find Christianity a stumbling block, it may be because they no longer listen to the voice of their nature but only to the sound of theories and research.

Original Sin and Noble Savages

Why do primitive people feel this need to be reborn? The

answer is that they feel unfinished, incomplete. Something about their present lives is unsatisfactory, even unsavory. They want a new start. "Whatever I am," wrote G. K. Chesterton, "I know I am not what I ought to be." When you read about the religions of primitive people or talk to those who have studied them, you find that he was voicing a fairly universal sentiment. Eliade says that primitive man, "wants to be other than he finds himself."

Why? Because in almost all societies you find a notion equivalent to the Christian belief in original sin, the idea that somewhere near the beginning something went very badly wrong with human beings so that human nature fell below the level of its original creation. Prior to this fall, man was in harmony both with himself and with God or the gods. Eliade calls this "the Myth of the Golden Age" and reports evidence of it in nearly every culture. The point, or at least one of the points, of the initiation ceremony is to die to the fallen profane self and to be born to a new life, a life where a man might once again have contact with the sacred, and thus fulfill his true nature.

One may call this superstition: that is a legitimate reaction. But it is not legitimate to pretend it is not there. This, I am afraid, is what a good many people, including scholars who ought to know better, do. Back in the eighteenth century when very little was known about anthropology, Europeans titillated themselves with the notion of the Noble Savage. They speculated that primitive people, being closer to the natural state, would be free of guilt and discontent. Along with this went the idea that primitive man, unlike his European counterpart, was happy doing whatever came naturally.

The idea is still remarkably popular, and perhaps nowhere more so than among psychologists of the humanistic school who are forever coaxing us to get in touch with our natural selves. This usually means we are to drop all our inhibitions, restraints, and prohibitions, and to model ourselves after natives in sarongs who are naively assumed to have no inhibitions or prohibitions. In this view, which may be called "The New Myth of the Golden Age," primitive people such as American Indians and New Guinea tribesmen are pictured as paragons of wholeness and harmony because they know how to live the natural (i.e., uninhibited) life; they have learned to accept themselves as they are.

From what we have just seen, this is an erroneous view. No actual "savage" believes in the myth of the Noble Savage—or, if he does, he believes that all the noble ones lived long ago in the Golden Age before the Fall, and he wishes he could be like them. Living the natural life, if it means just accepting your human condition as you find it and not striving to be born again to a supernatural plane, is something that the real primitive is not interested in. On casual acquaintance he may seem to take life as it comes, but you will find him suddenly quite serious when initiation time rolls around. When that comes, do not try to get him to act as you think he ought naturally to act, and be very careful to observe all the prohibitions and restraints; and do not, I beg of you, go near the segregated huts!

Like the Christian, primitive man thinks there is something wrong with his nature. So in primitive societies, just as in Christianity, we find this desire to put away the old self and begin everything anew. Often the candidate for initiation will be given a new name to signify both his new identity and the death of his former self. If you tell him instead that all he really needs is a better self-concept, he will listen carefully—politeness is a mark of maturity in most tribal societies—but he won't believe a word of it.

[95]

"God in a Bottle"

But we needn't go to the ends of the earth to find people who aren't pleased with the self they were born with; a walk down certain of our city streets will usually turn up any number of discontents. It is sometimes frightening to see them—the runaways, the alcoholics, the addicts, the prostitutes, the pornography seekers—but they have a lesson to teach us. Thoreau said that most men "lead lives of quiet desperation." Here we see a louder desperation. What are they desperate for? The answer is transcendence. They need to get *away* from something, away from boredom, routine, frustration, bad relationships, or loneliness. And they need to get *to* something, something powerful, extraordinary, exciting; something, in short, to lift them out of everyday life.

The attraction of the transcendent state is nicely illustrated in Thomas Wolfe's novel *Look Homeward Angel*. In one passage he describes his first experience with drunkenness.

> . . . It was, he knew, one of the great moments in his life. . . . In all the earth there was no other like him, no other fitted to be so sublimely and magnificently drunken. It was greater than all the music he had ever heard; it was as great as the highest poetry. Why had he never been told? Why had no one ever written adequately about it? Why, when it was possible to buy a god in a bottle, and drink him off, and become a god oneself, were men not forever drunken?[2]

But, of course, do-it-yourself transcendence can easily get out of hand. The god in the bottle turns out to be a powerful genie from the netherworld with a mind of his own. Before long the experimenter is in need of a rescue attempt, though, indeed, he may be reluctant to be rescued. But how to rescue him?

I sometimes ask my students, many of whom look forward to careers in the helping professions, what they will have to offer—say, to the alcoholic—that's better than "god in a bottle." Their answers tend to be framed along psychological lines: "adjustment to society," "coping," "a better self-concept," and so forth. Those responses, it seems to me, miss the point. If you can have god in a bottle, and temporarily be a god yourself, why would you settle for such paltry things as adjustment or coping? Once you have tasted transcendence, even the spurious kind, it is no easy matter to come back to earth.

The same is true for the experience of god in a hypodermic needle or god in an LSD tablet or god in the form of promiscuous or perverted sexuality. These things may be damaging to both body and soul, but they provide an intensity that is not readily found in everyday life. Do not imagine (I tell my students) that the care and concern given in your role as social worker or counselor will be an easy substitute for communion with the gods—even if they are only pagan gods.

A New Self

When these people—the addicts, alcoholics, and deviants of our society—finally come to the point where they want a change, they do not want a tune-up or some adjustments made on their selves. More often they want a brand new self. They consider their old self too badly damaged for repairs: they want to be rid of it. They see their lives as irremediably spoiled: they want a chance at a new one.

The psychological approach is usually not of much help in such cases because it deals not in conversions but in repairs. I am not saying it never works with these people, but what works more often is the type of organized community that demands submission, discipline, and faith and offers in return the chance once again at transcendence. Thus, the Black Muslims have been very successful at turning around the thwarted lives of broken men in the ghetto. And thus, Synanon, which demanded complete submission to the will of its charismatic leader, Chuck Diederick, proved far more successful at rehabilitating addicts than government programs based on psychological models.

Obviously there are dangers here, as the disastrous history of Synanon proves. But the point is this: very often the only thing that is better than god in a bottle is another god, one who is powerful enough to give you a new self. Or God. The Christian churches also have their share of ex-addicts, ex-criminals, and ex-prostitutes; and this is especially true of the more demanding forms of Christianity.

Christians hold that these wretched people are only a more dramatic example of the situation we are all in. We really do, all of us, need to turn away from our former selves because God wants us to be a new kind of person. There is even a respectable Christian tradition which maintains that these outcasts and misfits are, in a sense, more fortunate than the rest of us. They know how badly off they are, how much in need of a new birth. That is why respectable people need to be reminded that the publicans and sinners are entering the kingdom of heaven before them. We, if we are protected by our stable routines, or habits of moderation, or good mental health, can easily deceive ourselves into thinking we are doing just fine and that, if anything, all we need is a bit more self-awareness here or a tad more integration there.

The Spiritual Needs of Psychologists

If a slight mid-course correction is all you think you need, then you may well profit from what the psychological world has to offer. You shouldn't be surprised, however, if you find that it is not enough for your psychologist. For many psychologists, adjustment to ordinary life seems to be the thing furthest from their minds. On the contrary, there has always been a mystical streak in psychology.

I doubt whether the average person realizes how deep and wide that streak is or that it touches some of the most prominent names in psychology. Carl Jung, for example, centered his theory in an esoteric religious tradition; Wilhelm Reich suffered from messianic delusions; Erich Fromm was strongly inclined to Buddhist thought; Abraham Maslow concentrated his later writings on religion and peak experiences. This "religious" tradition in psychology carries down to some of the most respected and influential present-day psychologists. The attempt to get beyond the ordinary seems, for instance, now to be the main concern of both Carl Rogers and Elisabeth Kubler-Ross, both of whom report having contacted spirits of the dead.

From some sectors of psychology, it is true, this type of thing is looked on with embarrassment. But it is simply too widespread for the psychological community to do much about. In the event of a heresy trial, half the congregation would have to be excommunicated. Thus, one may attend a convention of psychologists, as I did once, where participants talk credulously of astral projection, reincarnation, the nonreality of matter, and "the transcendent spirit of oneness."

Much of the philosophy behind this is muddled and amateurish. But it does prove one point: in and of itself, psychology is not a satisfactory vision. Here are experts who have access to the most sophisticated and rational analysis psychology has to offer, and they prefer instead to practice yoga and meditation and consult with mediums and gurus.

This growing "spiritual" trend within psychology can be taken as a further corroboration of the point with which I began this chapter. It pays Christianity the compliment of admitting what Christians have maintained all along: we need to get ourselves on a different level.

Born-Again Psychology

It is not surprising, then, that psychology would sooner or later also come up with its own version of the born-again experience. The best example of this is the encounter group, with its remarkable claim of exchanging old lives for new and the equally remarkable emotionalism that attends it. It is as if a camp meeting were whisked out from its tent and set down in an upholstered conference room, and the preacher transformed by some sleight of hand into a group leader.

In encounter groups people confess their sins, share fellowship, claim to feel the workings of the spirit, and come out anxious to convert others to their way. In addition to encounter groups are the countless self-help books, pamphlets, and advertisements that promise new life, new personality, and psychological rebirth. They beat upon the brain like the noise of breakers and carry a similar force. Minds are swept before these promises like pebbles in surf. And, like a determined surfer, the mind keeps going back for more.

One thing, I think, is certain: when wrapped in the garments of psychology, the idea of being born again takes on a respectability that is not granted to Christian belief. The psychological society can believe what it wants with impunity. Sensing this, Christians will sometimes strive for a similar relevancy in the presentation and practice of the faith. But whether "the spirit" that animates these psychological conversions is related to the Holy Spirit is a question Christians must carefully ponder. Some Christians have been too quick to notice the similarities between Christianity and born-again psychology, and too slow to notice the differences, with the result that many church activities have taken on a distinctively "encounter group" flavor. And group methods have begun to substitute for Christian practice.

There are traps laid here for the unwary Christian, and one of them is the mistaken notion that spiritual progress is basically a matter of holding hands and hugging and feeling good about people. That is not what Christ meant when He instructed Nicodemus to be born again.

Even supposing the claims for radical personality change to be true, we must remember that encounter is still nothing more than secular salvation. It does not usher us into the kingdom of heaven. The same applies to the more modest goals of professional psychology: adjustment, personality integration, better functioning. Good things, yes. But you can have them and still be no better off in the eyes of heaven than a man mumbling lunacies in an asylum.

CHAPTER 8

Moral Education

One task of this book is to distinguish Christianity from psychological imitations of it. Now, an imitation is usually easy to spot when it is held up to the original. You can see that it is made of cheaper materials and hasn't been fastened together as strongly. But if you don't have the original at hand, you might be fooled into thinking the imitation is just as good. Sometimes Christians forget what Christianity is all about and begin to accept substitutes that can be produced at less cost and seem to perform the same functions.

One current example of this is the use by Christians of moral education programs developed by secular psychologists. In the United States and Canada the two most popular programs are the "values clarification" approach and the "moral reasoning" approach. Educators who use these programs have the benefit of prepackaged kits and an abundance of stimulating material—and, of course, the stamp of scientific psychology.

These approaches have become immensely popular, not only in public schools but also in Christian ones. In some religious education programs they seem to be offered as a surer guide to morality than prayer or the Ten Commandments. Other Christians, however, along with conservative Jews, have criticized these programs as being anti-religious in nature.

Who Is Right?

The question arises as to who is right: those Christians who wholeheartedly adopt the new techniques or those who wholeheartedly reject them? Those who reject them are open to the charge of quibbling. If someone is working toward the same goal as you, why quarrel over his methods? If the man next to you is doing his best to bail out the boat, why criticize him for bailing to port rather than to starboard?

This, I think, is the reasoning of those Christians who support the new psychological techniques for moral education and values clarification. "It may not be perfect," they say, "but at least it's on the right track. At least it gets young people to think about values—and that's the important thing." This attitude may be called the moral-of-the-story approach. The inventors of the new techniques, it is argued, may not buy the Bible story, but when you look closely you see that what they are working toward turns out to have the same moral message.

I can illustrate this attitude by mentioning a colleague, a non-Christian psychologist who happens to run workshops in values clarification techniques. He likes to insist that he and I have the same basic values. Our beliefs are not that different, he maintains. He thinks of himself as a Christian with a small "c." He believes in justice, compassion, and loving one's neighbor, and he recognizes the importance of family values and individual responsibility. He is very tolerant of Christianity since he looks on it as merely a variation, though not to his taste, of his own agenda for making the world a better place.

Once, though, he got involved in a discussion with me and three other Christians and found to his chagrin that what we believed was not at all what he had thought. His face reddened and stayed that way during the entire conversation. I had never seen him so uncomfortable. He looked like a man who had come to dinner in a sportcoat only to find the others dressed in tuxedos.

We tend to forget how very different a thing Christianity is—how decisively and uncomfortably different. The consequence of maintaining that distinction is so threatening all around that people on both sides of the Christian fence will take pains to cover up the difference. My colleague knows other Christians, of course, but they are Christians who are anxious to show how much their beliefs are in tune with the rest of the world's. When he stumbled into our conversation, he did not know what he was letting himself in for.

He thought (and still thinks) one can have Christianity without bothering too much about Christ or the Christian story. This is a widespread belief. Many think the essence of Christianity is an ethical message. Originally, according to this view, the message was cast in the form of stories suited to the understanding of illiterate farmers and fishermen. The important thing, however, is to grasp the ethical principle, the moral of the story. Once you have that, you can dispense with the story itself. The story is just the ribboned box in which the present comes. It follows, then, that for moderns the ethical message might be wrapped in a completely different box or no box at all.

All of this seems wrongheaded to me, but before going into the reasons why, you must allow me to make a detour into the past.

The Traditional Approach to Morality: Four Rules

One point I have stressed is that psychology doesn't understand human nature nearly so well as it thinks. There is a deeper psychology that was once understood not only by

Christians but by all people everywhere. It didn't require elaborate theorizing because it was simply what people had found to be true, generation after generation. Just as you learned that you had better not nail too close to the edge or you would split the wood, and just as you learned to slope your roofs in a northern country, you also learned that human beings ought to act thus and so or else certain consequences would follow.

Take this matter of moral education. Our ancestors, whether they were Christian or not, believed four things about teaching morality:

1. There was a right way to behave and a wrong way.
2. You learned the right way by being trained in it.
3. You also needed models of virtue to imitate.
4. These models could be found in stories of wisdom and courage.

Let us look at the good sense of this. First, there is a right way to behave. Can we prove this? No, not strictly. You cannot prove that friendship, loyalty, courage, honesty, and justice are better than betrayal, treachery, cowardice, deceit, and injustice. But then neither can you prove that a roof that doesn't leak is better than one that does. People with common sense don't try to prove it. In fact, it is usually a mistake to try to prove the obvious. Think of the parent who foolishly tries to give a logical case against dishonesty every time her toddler tells a lie. The case against it is not logical but definitional. Good boys and girls do not lie.

Second: you learned to do the right thing by being trained in it. It isn't enough to know how to play tennis from reading a manual. You have to practice it. Virtue, too, must be practiced until it becomes habitual. It has to be in the "muscles" as much as in the mind. It is all to the good to have a handy set of moral principles; but unless you are accustomed to putting them into practice, they won't be of much use when a difficult moral test comes. When such tests come, they do not arrive under ideal circumstances. When we are tired, angry, or afraid, or when the temptation is overwhelmingly attractive, it is more prudent for us to rely on our training than on our good intentions. A moral situation, as our ancestors understood, is more like a physical struggle than a mental problem. If we have been educated properly, we respond like a trained boxer who, when attacked, automatically blocks and counterpunches. Without training, we will end up more often than not flat on our backs. (The similarity between the two types of training explains, by the way, why it is often maintained that playing sports builds character.)

Third: you need training in the virtues, but you also need models to imitate. Training is demanding. We need something to keep us at it, something to motivate us. In the abstract we know that virtue is its own reward and that we should be good simply because it is good to be good. But we seem to require more. Here again, athletic training provides an analogy. It should be enough for the aspiring gymnast to know that gymnastic exercises are worth doing in and for themselves. Done well, they have a natural grace and power that few other activities can match. But what do we find if we look into the young gymnast's room? On the wall is a poster of the Olympic champion, and over there are more pictures cut out of magazines, and on the desk are stories and clippings about heroes of the gymnastic world. When we have someone to identify with, someone we admire, and someone who does what we do, only better, we have found ourselves something to train toward. It is, of course, the same with character training. Virtue is its own reward, but we need moral models to make it seem worthwhile on our way toward it. We need someone to tell us, "Here is what good people do; here is what heroic people do"; and even, "Here is what exciting people do. If you want to be like them, do likewise."

This brings us to the fourth point and explains why the chief means of moral education in classical and heroic societies was the telling of stories. Long before the Greeks learned their ethics from Aristotle, they learned them from *The Iliad* and *The Odyssey*. Here are Achilles and Odysseus and Hector and Penelope. Here they are acting well, and here they are not. This is the way the Greeks approached moral education; the Romans, the Irish, and the Icelanders did the same. Later on, when Christianity swept the world, it was the gospel story, not the Christian ethic, that captured men's hearts. Still later, people learned how to behave well by hearing accounts of the lives of saints and stories of Arthur, Percival, and Gallahad.

A Life Is a Story

Our ancestors went even further. Not only are stories good teaching devices but our own lives are best understood as stories. This certainly is the implication of all those passages in *The Iliad* where Achilles and Odysseus and the others seem unable to identify themselves to strangers without bringing in the whole family history. There is no possibility here of imagining oneself as a self-made individual. An individual is more than just an individual self. He belongs to an ongoing tradition, a family story or a tribal story. He says, in effect, "I am defined by the story of which I am a part." His line of descendants is also his story line.

J.R.R. Tolkien captured this in *The Lord of the Rings*. We hear Aragorn, for example, introducing himself as, "Aragorn, son of Arathorn, the heir of Isildur, Elendil's son of Gondor. Here is the Sword that was broken and is forged again." Everyone, of course, is expected to know the story of The Sword and of Isildur and Elendil. The characters in *The Rings* live and breathe stories.

The popularity of Tolkien's work suggests that we moderns are not past needing stories. People read Tolkien not because he provides escape—any number of books do that—but because he speaks to deep human needs. It is the sheer humanness of the characters, even the nonhuman ones, that appeals. They know how to live, and we are not sure anymore that we do. They are aware of the stories to which they belong. We are not at all sure of the point of our lives or what part we are meant to play. Yet despite ourselves, we all want and need to play a part. You can see this in children's play. Much of it consists in inventing dramas, assigning roles, and acting them out. You can see it in the adult's need to convince himself and others that the work he does is a useful part of a larger endeavor. No one wishes to consider that his life might be pointless. The reason we love biography above almost every literary form is that it holds out the promise that a life can be made into something like a story.

I hope this talk of stories does not seem fanciful. Try to make sense of your life from any other perspective and see if you can. Humanism does not make a good story, neither does scientism or psychology. None of them can make any sense out of our lives. That is, none of them can tell us anything about the purpose of our lives. From any of these points of view, we are all replaceable. Note, however, that once a character has been put into a story, he is not replaceable. The author cannot introduce him and then drop him without damaging the narrative. Once you are in the story, you become necessary to it.

The Part You Play

We must remember, though, that we cannot expect to see the whole sense of our lives at every step of the way. That does not mean there is no sense. To the character in a story, the events that befall him on page 51 may make no sense whatever, but we the readers, because we see the several parts and strands of the story, can see that there is a sense to it. Take, for example, a thriller such as *Eye of the Needle*. The story moves back and forth from one sub-plot to another. There is the Nazi spy who has uncovered the plans for the D-Day invasion; there is the British intelligence officer who means to thwart him; there is the young unhappy couple living out a seemingly meaningless life on a North Sea Island. We see the various strands of the story slowly, and then quite rapidly, coming together. We see the part each is to play. But the woman on the island has no idea, until the very end, of the significance of the part she plays. Indeed, for most of the story her life appears to her as increasingly pointless and plotless. Yet finally, her part turns out to have been the most crucial. Her life story intersects with the lives of millions in Europe and Britain.

When we read a story like this, we are tempted to say, "If only I could play an important part like that, then all the rest would have been worth it." But who says that you do not? If you are only on page 51, you cannot expect to see all the strands of your story. You cannot know how it will turn out or fully understand what part you have been playing. Perhaps it will turn out to have been a very crucial part.

It is the point of Christianity that we each do play an irreplaceable part in a cosmic drama, a story in which some of the strands only come together in eternity. In such a story, what you do counts infinitely. But even non-

Christians and pre-Christians have shared this sense of storied lives. They all believed that the best incentive to moral behavior was this conviction that we are part of a story that begins before us and goes on after us, but whose outcome we may influence.

The important thing, then, is to play our part well. In various times and places this might be called doing your duty, or keeping a stiff upper lip, or not letting others down. Under it all, however, was the conviction of some ongoing enterprise to which all belonged. To be sure, there was more to moral education than this, but the foundation of it had to do with this notion that in order to have character you needed to be a character—a character bound to a particular story.

Let us not think that this view was always a cause for rejoicing in the ancient world. For there are sad stories and tragic stories, and they were well aware of this. Acting well was no guarantee of anything: fate might at any time step in and play her part in the story. Still, these people seemed to prefer even that to the idea that life had no narrative whatever.

Although I happen to believe this view of our lives is essentially correct, I point it out here simply as a psychological fact. When we go back to the time before man alienated himself from his nature, this is what we find. A great persistent voice from Homer to Mallory and beyond gives witness to it. If you will not take account of it, your psychology will be impoverished.

The Modern Approach to Teaching Values

The modern world thinks it has grown up and does not need stories. When you have your heart set on autonomy, as much of our society does, stories can only be seen as limiting and confining. We prefer to think of the self not as a character-in-a-story but as a character-at-large bound to nothing but its own development. And this is the view that the new psychological programs of moral education encourage.

We do not need to go into the background of this movement. Let it suffice to say that the new psychological solution began by rejecting the past out of hand. It was decided that although students were to be encouraged to think about values, they must be free to choose. No indoctrination should take place, no set of values should be given priority. Tolerance for other points of view should prevail. Like so many other things, morality was to be entrusted to the democratic decision-making process.

I am sure you are aware of this approach. In values clarification the usual strategy is to ask a student to rank in order from a list of values those that he most likes and dislikes. Although there are variations, that is pretty much as far as it goes. In the end it is the student's own personal preference that determines right and wrong.

The moral reasoning approach is more sophisticated: although one can never say what is right or wrong, one can develop better moral reasoning and eventually discover universal ethical principles. The general technique here is the discussion of moral dilemmas: Should a man steal food to save his starving wife? Is it permissible for passengers in a foundering lifeboat to throw others overboard? Should an older sister lie to cover up her younger sister's disobedience? Discussions of this sort are meant to prod students into sharpening their moral judgment. It should be added that all these discussions are conducted in a neutral fashion: the teacher must refrain from taking sides.

The main thing to notice here is the absence of those things our ancestors thought important for moral education. There is no suggestion that right and wrong can actually be known, no training in virtue, no models to imitate, and finally, no stories. Although I wish to concentrate on the last two, it might be useful to list several preliminary objections.

Objections to the New Approach

1. Traditional morality is at a disadvantage from the outset. The ground rules set down by the value educators insist on a nonjudgmental attitude. If you happen to believe in the distinction between right and wrong, you must leave it at the door. This amounts to saying, "Concede our major premise, and then we will begin the argument." Although it is all wrapped up in high-sounding talk about impartiality, it is really no different from the man who invites you to come into the boxing ring with one arm tied behind your back.

2. A nonjudgmental approach undermines any character training that may have taken place. Education in virtue is in part an *education sentimentale*. The heart is trained as well as the mind so that the virtuous person learns not only to distinguish between good and evil but to love the one and hate the other. The idea that all things are open to discussion and all values are welcome in the classroom is a subtle form of conditioning that deprives us of our inbred repugnance to vice or debased values. Evenhanded, dispassionate discussions erode moral sentiments and habituate students to the notion that moral questions are merely intellectual problems rather than human problems that ought to call up strong emotions. The proper response to a house guest who attempts to seduce your wife is to send him packing, not to discuss with him the merits of seduction.

3. The concentration on moral dilemmas puts the cart before the horse. Before students begin to think about the qualifications, exceptions, and fine points that surround difficult cases they will seldom or never face, they need to build the kind of character that will allow them to act well in the very clear-cut situations they face daily. If you are thinking of taking a boat on a pond, a course in sailing will serve you much better than one on celestial navigation. The great danger of the open-ended method of moral education is that students will come away with the impression that morality is not a solid and obvious thing but a series of quandaries subject to innumerable interpretations and qualifications. From here, of course, it is only a short step to finding the appropriate provisos and saving clauses necessary to make one's own conscience comfortable in all situations.

4. In other crucial matters we do not wait upon our child's free choice before training him in good habits. Why should we do so, then, in matters of morality, which are, after all, far more important than learning to brush one's teeth or button one's coat? We would be shocked to find a parent who left it up to the child to find out for himself that playing in the street is a dangerous thing. May we not be at least as surprised at educators who allow children to devise their own moral content? You will not find this method in any other field of education. A good science teacher, for example, may sometimes use an inquiry method, but his students are not simply left to themselves to discover what Galileo, Newton, and Einstein discovered. There are laws of physics, chemistry, and mathematics that any conscientious teacher will want to teach and not simply leave up to chance.

5. To know the good is not necessarily to do the good. It is naive to suppose that once we have clarified a value or made a proper moral judgment we will then act accordingly. The

hard part of morality lies in actually doing the thing we know to be right. It is reasonable to ask why contemporary moral educators have not seen this. The answer is twofold. On the one hand they have a great faith in education, and on the other they have a great trust in human nature. By and large they are bound to the theory that there is no such thing as a bad boy, only an ignorant one. That is why their whole effort is bent toward getting the boy to think for himself—something he presumably has never done before. This is the same attitude that supposes that driver education will prevent accidents, that alcohol education will prevent drunkenness, and that sex education will prevent venereal disease. They do not. And neither does modern moral education prevent immorality. The problem with human beings is not simply a lack of education.

Now, back to stories.

The Moral of the Story:
The Line Without the Hook

Earlier in this chapter I promised to take up in more detail the attitude which says that as long as you have the moral of the story you don't need the story itself. This is the attitude of many Christians who ally themselves with psychological programs, and I now propose to deal with it. What is wrong with this idea is the same thing that is wrong with a fishing line that has no hook. You do not get to the essence of a fishing line by removing the irrelevant barb on the end of it. When you do that, you have taken away the "grab" of the thing. In the same way, when you take away the story you take away most of the motivation for doing the good deed. The moral principle has lost its grab.

It is not enough to comprehend a moral situation, you

must also care about it; and it is one of the peculiarities of the moral dilemma approach that it lacks any power to make us care. The characters in the dilemmas are cardboard cut-outs. We have no interest in them, only in their case. The dilemmas are stories of a kind, but they are dehydrated stories. There is no juice in them. One cannot imagine parents passing down to their children the "Saga of the Starving Wife and the Stolen Food." A dilemma—still less a neutral values discussion—provides no model of virtue for us to follow. A young person might very well be able to derive some valid moral principles from discussions of these cases, but a principle is a good deal less than half the moral equation.

Test this for yourself by recalling a difficult moral situation in which you acted rightly. You will see first off that, in most instances, the hard thing was not knowing what was right but doing it. Second, you asked yourself not, "What is the principle involved here?" but something more like: "What would others think of me if they found I acted this way? What would my parents think? My wife? My children? My friends?"

Almost automatically you began to envision yourself as an actor in a drama. The important question became, "Will I play my role well or will I fail in it?' I know that the thing that prods me to act as I know I should works in just this way. Ethical principles? Yes, I've done the required reading. But I find that when the chips are down, almost anything—a mental image of friends or family, a memory of a story or film, a simple sense of duty—is stronger than that. I am well aware that there are highly principled people who seem to be able to act from principle alone. I salute them. But I do not think most people operate that way. I know I do not. Let me give a specific example

The Parable of the Naked Man and the Tire Iron

The naked man appeared in my headlights one very cold winter night on a darkened street. He was wearing only pajama tops, and he was frantically waving me to stop. It is curious how many thoughts can pass through one's mind in a few seconds. The first thought I had was that I simply did not want to stop. It had been a bad day for me already. Besides, whatever was going on here was not my problem. Let someone else stop. Moreover, it looked like a potentially dangerous situation. The man could be a lunatic. If I stopped to help, I might get hurt. If I should get seriously hurt, what good would I be to those who depend on me? Oh yes, I realized that ethical principles were involved. And I had no doubt that some moral rule or other required me to stop or do something. But at the moment my mind was nimbly inventing qualifications, loopholes, and exceptions to whatever moral law applied. I might feel bad for a while afterward, but I've found you can get over that. Let the police handle it.

Then a sentence from a story inexplicably passed into my head: "Clothe the naked." Nothing else. Just, "Clothe the naked."

I stopped.

The man as it turned out had awakened to the sounds of a housemate-gone-berserk who was smashing furniture with a tire iron. When the housemate turned on this man, he wasted no time worrying about his dignity and fled for his life. After hearing his hurried explanation, I quickly found a blanket for him in the car and we sped off to a nearby police station. The point I wish to make is simply this: I did not stop on principle. I stopped because the hero of a story I believe in once said, "Clothe the naked." I stopped because He would have stopped and those of us who believe this story want very much to imitate Him, even if ours is a poor imitation.

Note that the gospel story does not say, "Clothe the naked because all people are invested with human dignity" or "Clothe the naked because justice demands it"; just, "Clothe the naked." Period. Do it because this is what is expected of those who want to play a part in the Christian story.

The main reason—and it is a difficult one for non-Christians to grasp—that you cannot extract ethical principles from Christianity and set them up on their own is that Christianity is *not* an ethical system. It is not meant to be a prescription for good behavior, although good behavior is one of its side effects. It is a story. Christians believe that it is a true story but a story, nonetheless.

Christianity Without Christ?

When you see this, you can begin to understand why it makes no sense to talk about keeping the Christian ethic and ignoring Christ. The story is mainly about Christ: who He is and what He has done. Without Him it makes no sense, just as, if you will excuse the comparison, the story of *Moby Dick* makes no sense without the driven personality of Ahab. Many of the things Christians do—good works, sacrifices, disciplines—they do for no ethical reason and sometimes for no earthly reason. They do them because they want to follow Christ.

You cannot separate the message of Christ from the person of Christ and simply pretend that His words could be put into any good person's mouth. How would it sound if any other man, even a great man, were to talk about himself the way Christ did? How would it sound if Winston Churchill had said, "I am the Resurrection and the Life?" Or if George Washington had said, "Before Abraham came to be, I Am?"

That is not their story. Those lines belong to only one Person.

Some Further Points

One or two further points remain to be raised. Given a situation like the one I found myself in, suppose you stop your car and it turns out the tire iron is meant for you? What will you think about it afterwards, provided your brain hasn't been too badly battered to think? The answer to that is, of course, that morality does not exclude prudence: the judicious sizing-up of a situation. That is one answer. The other is that both stories and lives have tragic events. Doing the right thing is no guarantee that good consequences will follow. The fact is, often we simply do not know what the aftermath of our actions will be. What we can see are the obvious duties to neighbor, friend, or family. Our role is to play our part faithfully and as best as we can see it, not to foresee the future.

If we balk at this, it is because we want morality to be more like a science than a story. We are looking for some universal viewpoint divorced from all particular stories, a place from which we may exercise our autonomous judgment of affairs. We would like to be able to foresee all consequences and predict all outcomes. But that is a foolish attitude. None of us is ever afforded such a vantage point.

The other thing to notice is this: the more abstract your ethic, the less power it has to move you. When we do act decently, it is usually local loves and loyalties—the kind that make for a good story—that account for it; that, or an actual story to which we feel bound. Take those away and replace them with a detached and neutral love for all mankind, and you will usually make a person worse, not better. People who nourish themselves purely on principle are notorious for sacrificing loyalties and even lives on the altar of "mankind" or "brotherhood." When you are tempted to mistreat another, you are better off to remember that he, like you, is someone's brother or father or son than to think of his essential human rights. Or from the Christian point of view, you are better to remember that Christ also died for him.

At present, three approaches to moral education vie for our attention: the values clarification approach, the moral reasoning approach, and the traditional approach. The first is a morality of personal preference—"what I like is right"—and is therefore really no morality at all. The second is a morality of rules and reasoning. It has some merit, but it diverts our attention from the real moral arena. The third is a morality of character. It gives us good people as models and asks us to act like them; it provides us with stories to live by.

My contention is that the last of these is the best because life is more like that. Life is full and rich and complex like a story, not abstract and neat like a theory. The things that happen to us—the great joys, the intense sorrows, the surging passions—are too much like drama to be accounted for by anything less than drama. Sometimes it may seem that it is too much like a story: too uncertain, too unbearably tragic. At such times I think we are tempted to wish that, instead of a story, God had given us something more like an amusement park to live in. We could then have the illusion of adventure—the thrills and spills—without the danger. We want a place where the terrors are only mock terrors like the terrors of the House of Horrors. But I doubt we would be satisfied with all the corollaries.

Much further than that I cannot go. The argument is in the realm of imagination, not logic. What needs to be seen is that virtue in large part is also in the realm of imagination. Unless the moral imagination is hooked, the other moral faculties—will, emotion, and reason—are too often over-matched by fear, laziness, and self-interest. The great mistake of modern psychology lies in ignoring this obvious fact while it toys with values clarification and decision-making exercises. That is why I believe that our ancestors, both Christian and non-Christian, were the better psychologists. They knew that you must grasp the imagination, and they knew how to do it.

A Distinctive Identity

A final point. Our stories give us a distinctive identity, and partly because of this we are under constant outside pressure to forget them. The great temptation for a storied people is to blend with the world and accept its story, which is usually that there is no story, only progress or scientific fact or evolutionary necessity.

Our stories allow us to stand back from the rest of the world and judge its claim. Without them, we lose that ability; instead of assessing claims, we accede to them. As I write this, for instance, the news is full of the British victory in the Falkland Islands off Argentina. To the citizens of Argentina the defeat came as a great shock, for their government-controlled press had led them to believe they were winning the war. Most of the people in that country had no way to check the official version or to question it. What can happen with news stories can happen also with life stories. You can be left with only one version of reality. It is important, therefore, for a storied people to keep their story fresh in mind for, despite their claims to the contrary, modern societies do

usually have a story line they are anxious to push on us—
either Marxism or humanism or consumer hedonism.

Stanley Hauerwas, a philosopher to whom I am indebted
for making so much of this clear to me, has observed that, "to
be trained to resist the state requires nothing less than an
alternative story and society in which the self can find a
home."[1] Certainly this is borne out today in Poland where
resistance to the communist state is possible because the
people have not forgotten to which story they belong.

But there are more subtle ways of subverting our beliefs
than armed occupation, as we shall see.

CHAPTER 9

The Dismal Science:
1984 and Beyond

In a scene in C. S. Lewis's *The Silver Chair*, the beautiful witch/queen of the Underworld nearly convinces the children from the Overworld that her own rather dismal kingdom is the only reality, and theirs but an imagined dream. Her cunning use of words acts like a drug on their memory.

The children feel vaguely that there is something of great importance they must remember. Indeed there is. They have been sent on a mission by Aslan, the great King of Narnia. But at the moment, all they can think of is the *thrum-thrum-thrum* of the Queen's mandolin and her lulling voice. "The sun? There is no sun. You have seen my lamps and imagined that there was a sun." That is her subtle yet convincing suggestion.

Earlier in the story, Aslan had given them four signs to remember and repeat. With the signs came a caution: "—the signs which you have learned here will not look at all as you expect them to look . . . that is why it is so important to know them by heart and pay no attention to appearances." But now they have forgotten the signs and Aslan as well. Appearances have become everything to them. The Queen, after all, is quite beautiful.

Lewis takes up an ancient theme here: the importance —and the difficulty—of remembering. Odysseus, you will remember, has that problem. He's supposed to be heading back to his homeland, to his wife and son. But everything conspires to make him forget. Again and again he and his men are put to the test of memory: on the island of the Lotus Eaters where those who ate "the honeyed plant" longed "to stay forever . . . forgetful of their homeland"; on Circe's enchanted island where they lingered for a fatted year; before the Sirens whose song "sings the mind away from children and from wife"; and last of all by the beautiful Calypso.

Aeneas, the hero of Virgil's epic, has a similar habit of almost forgetting the main point. It takes a messenger from the gods to remind him that his mission is to found his new city in Italy not in Carthage. Still, Aeneas is a hero because he does not, when all is said and done, forget. His chief virtue is in remembering to be faithful to his ruined homeland.

Almost all epics and many fairy tales involve journeys, and there is always something to be kept in mind while on the journey. Or else there are stories to be faithfully handed down—stories about the old times when the true kings ruled, the time before the usurpers. Unless the stories are told and retold, they will be forgotten. When that happens, the pretenders will have captured both body and mind. There will be only one version of history, one version of reality. In the Narnia tales we see great stress laid on this. The old stories, the ancient rhymes and sayings, are treasured and passed down in good times and in bad. Particularly in the bad times one needs every device to recall what was true because a new "truth" reigns, and it works to crowd out every competitor.

The great modern version of this theme is *1984*. A shoddy, dehumanized totalitarianism has replaced the free society of England, and almost no one realizes what has happened. The government has been busy changing the language:

dropping old words or changing their meanings or conceal-
ing meanings with a deliberate haze of slogans. So, in the
jargon of Newspeak, "War is Peace" and "Freedom is Slavery" and the government torture chambers are located in
"The Ministry of Love."

Why dwell on all this fiction? Well, for the same reason
Orwell did. It's not exactly all fiction. Some of it, indeed a
great deal of *1984*, was already a reality when Orwell wrote it.
The outline was quite plainly visible in Hitler's Germany
and Stalin's Russia: the rewriting of history, the erasure of
memory through brainwashing, the flagrant manipulation of
language. Thanks to Orwell, we are perhaps more on our
guard than we might have been against that sort of thing. But
the point of all these stories is that things "will not look at all
as you expect them to look." We must be alert to the possibility that the theft of our memory (and with it, of course, our
loyalty) will emanate from an unexpected quarter.

. . . Psychology, for instance.

The Pressure to Forget

Our transformation into a psychological society has
brought with it a new set of values. They are shallow and
selfish values for the most part, and they are the ruling
values. But that is not the worst side of the situation. The
disturbing thing is the very effective suppression of alterna-
tives. It is difficult to remember what the old values are, let
alone to pass them on.

Much of this suppression is accomplished by the manipulation and manufacture of words. Think of the phrases that
have recently slipped into the language: "communications
skills," "stress management," "conflict resolution," "group
process," "interpersonal dynamics," and so on. The first
thing we notice about this talk is that, like Newspeak, it is

singularly drab. The second thing we notice is that it's confusing. It seems to say in effect, "You don't have the expertise to understand these things; you'd better let us take charge." I find that this kind of talk always has a hypnotic effect on me. "The proposed program *(thrum)* is a synthesis *(thrum)* of values clarification and behavior modification *(thrum)* and the application of cybernetic models *(thrum)* for understanding the human as an information processing being *(thrum-thrum)*." The average person doesn't know what this means, but the speaker always seems to be quite sure of himself. And so, still in a trance, we tend to nod in agreement: "Yes, yes. If you think that's what we should be doing, then by all means apply, uhm, er, the cybernetic model."

Manipulating Reality

The manipulation of words, as Orwell realized, is also the manipulation of reality. If you call a certain deed "murder," it summons up one reality to the mind. Call it "pro-choice," and the reality seems different. This is often the effect of the social sciences on language. Meanings get turned on their heads. The man who assaults you is called a "victim." A woman who leaves her family is called "courageous." A couple who commit adultery are said to have an "open" marriage.

These are rather flagrant manipulations, but there are more subtle ones. Take the use of a term such as "parenting experience." It seems harmless enough. But is it? The words *mother* and *father* have powerful moral and emotional connotations. They speak to a world of family ties, demands, common goals, and mutual love. Images come to mind of babies in bassinets and family suppers and stringing ornaments on Christmas trees and helping out with homework and steering clear of father at income tax time. What images does "parenting experience" call to mind? What images is it meant to convey?

I suspect none. The words *mother* and *father* remind us of what a family ought to be and that without one we are incomplete. But this isn't a fashionable idea. Autonomous individuals have a higher priority than families in the social science world. And so "parenting experience" is the term of choice. It's more abstract and conjures up no images of strong emotional ties. It's an "experience" like any other experience you might want to try out on your road to actualization. Nothing final about it.

To advance the cause of the autonomous person, the old concepts and loyalties need to be forgotten. The old ideas that blood is thicker than water or that children should be obedient or that families ought to stick together must lose currency. But to accomplish that goal, language must be reworked into forms that are understood only by experts, forms that make you and me feel ignorant and, therefore, all the more susceptible to intervention. Most of us have some idea how to rear children, but how does one "parent" them?

Terms like these may be considered as only interim steps. After "parenting experience" has done its work of softening up the body politic, what comes next? The "adult-offspring experience"? "The reproducer-reproducee relationship"? It is no good saying that the words you use don't matter. They matter immensely. Try to imagine a world where people are addressed only by their numbers.

Weakening Loyalties

There are some ironies here, the chief one being that though the psychological society talks the language of freedom, it seems intent on doing the same kind of thing that police states do. The worst indecency of the totalitarian mind is that it wants to wipe out all special ties of emotion or allegiance such as might exist between husband and wife or parent and child. These kinds of loyalties threaten the only allegiance considered important, the one owed to Big Brother. It is in this atmosphere, of course, that children willingly denounce their parents to the secret police.

The business of the psychological society also seems to be the business of weakening loyalties. It's done in the name of personal independence, to be sure, but the result will be the same. The fact is that the breakdown of natural groupings usually heralds less freedom, not more. One thing you notice about totalitarian states is that they have little use for the family or the parish or the local government. They like nothing better than to liberate the individual from his local bonds. So we must be as wary of an excessive individualism as we are of collectivism. The one leads to the other. Look over your shoulder as you back away from those intrusive family members and those parish busybodies and see what you are backing into.

If we are headed toward any more individualism than we already have, we are headed in a mistaken direction. But the mistake is difficult to correct because it is so hard to spot in the first place. What we will be able to see is, as I have suggested, tied to the words and concepts available to us. If your attention is directed over here where the shouting and the slogans are, you might not notice that over there something of importance has quietly disappeared. One man creates a disturbance in this corner, and at the other end of the room his partner walks off with the silver.

It's like that with language. Language determines the realities we attend to. If certain words fall into desuetude, it means that certain realities have dropped from our attention as well. Words, for example, such as *valor, nobility, honor, sanctity, chastity,* and *purity* hang on to life but seem to be written in the past tense, as though the realities they refer to are remnants of some dim history. Such words appear rarely, if at all, in the vocabulary of social scientists or in the popular media. Other, more "relevant" words have edged them aside. For every *purity* that gets into print, there are a hundred *needs, naturals,* and *sexuals* to crowd it out.

What is perhaps most effective about such a technique is that it requires no confrontation. It does not deny the other realities. It by-passes them the way a superhighway by-passes a village so that after a while people forget that the village is there.

The Christian Story

Let us not forget that there is more to the world than psychological superhighways. Christians, especially, should not forget. The Christian story is the most astonishing version of reality ever imagined. Next to it, the other versions are monographs and ledger books. One would want to be very sure that it is only a myth before exchanging it for the slender story line offered by the psychological society. Yet the social scientists and their popularizers have been remarkably effective in making Christians forget. Many nominal Christians seem to have accepted the idea that it is somehow more interesting to be "a person" than it is to be an heir to a kingdom prepared from the beginning of time. Their situation is not unlike that of the children in Lewis's Underworld. For them the drab world of psychological ideas has nearly replaced the splendid realities of heaven and earth.

There are many things the secular/psychological world would like us to put out of mind. But let us concentrate on one of them. The story of Odysseus will be helpful in introducing it, for in this one particular we are very much (if you will excuse the pun) in the same boat with him. Like Odysseus we are invited to settle down on Circe's island (never mind that in our case it looks more like Orwell's Oceania) and forget. And by an odd but predictable irony we are being asked to forget the very same thing: that we are wanderers in search of our homeland.

Wanderers?

Consider the data. And I mean by data certain experiences that almost everyone shares in common. Most people at one time or another have had the conviction (or perhaps only the uneasy sensation) of not feeling quite at home in this world. This happens to you even when you *are* at home and even when home has all the coziness imaginable. I think everyone knows what I mean. You can come at this experience from two angles: the negative experience we all have of missing out on some important thing that we can't put our finger on, and the positive experience of feeling that, beyond all reason, something very important waits somewhere for us. The sense of the first is conveyed by Charles Dickens in a letter to a friend: "Why is it," he wrote at the pinnacle of his career, "that . . . a sense comes always crushing on me now, when I fall into low spirits, as of one happiness I have missed in life, and one friend and companion I have never made?" And Huxley wrote, "Sooner or later one asks even of Beethoven, even of Shakespeare, 'Is that all?'"

Lewis described the positive aspect of this desire as well as anyone has. He called it "the inconsolable longing."

You have never *had* it. All the things that have ever deeply possessed your soul have been but hints of it—tantalising glimpses, promises never quite fulfilled, echoes that died away just as they caught your ear. But if it should really become manifest—if there ever came an echo that did not die away but swelled into the sound itself—you would know it. Beyond all possibility of doubt you would say "Here at last is the thing I was made for."[1]

The joy of which Lewis speaks is not the joy of fulfillment or satisfaction, but rather the joy of unfulfillment: a glimpse of something farther off, "news from a country we have never visited." Whatever is there is gone as soon as it is found. Yet it bears down upon us the sense that we are living as exiles. For a moment our amnesia is lifted. Wherever home is, we feel we have not yet found it—and strangely we are glad.

The Desire That Won't Be Satisfied

Built into the very core of human nature is a desire that no natural happiness will satisfy and beside which other desires seem insignificant. We remain under the conviction that this—whatever we have—is not quite it. At the deepest level we find not the inner harmony which some psychologists profess to see, but a radical incompleteness: our whole nature seems anticipatory, preparatory.

There it is. You've experienced it. And you don't have to be a Christian or even a theist to experience it. Augustine had the experience long before his conversion. So did Lewis. Indeed, Lewis fought, kicking and struggling, against the possibility that the source of his longing and the God of traditional religion might be one and the same. Of his "search for God," Lewis said, "They might as well talk about the mouse's search for the cat."

The point is of some importance, for it brings the experience into the realm of natural phenomena. It falls into the category of data, a fact of human nature—the sort of thing psychologists are supposed to study and report on. But by-and-large they don't. Why? Because it fits none of the categories. There is no other desire or need quite like it. The others can be labeled, sorted, and explained, and then matched up with a suitable need fulfiller. But not this. And so, the psychologist is forced to make a detour around this mysterious area of our experience as though it weren't there.

The other tactic is to reduce the data to a manageable size. When they have no explanation for a phenomenon, psychologists often fit it into a category they do have an explanation for. It shouldn't be surprising if the phenomenon at hand gets a little damaged in the process. It's like trying to fit a size twelve shoe into a size four shoebox or trying to stuff a bird of paradise into a canary cage. Once you cram it in there, it won't look like a bird of paradise anymore.

So when the psychological society gets ahold of our yearning, it will want to explain it in terms of something it does understand (or thinks it understands), such as sexuality. This longing, they will say, is a sublimation of your need for sex. Or this homeland you're looking for is your mother's womb. It represents your need for security.

This is the tactic of the Underworld Queen: "You've seen cats, and now you want a bigger and better cat, and it's to be called a *lion*." "You have seen lamps and so you imagined a bigger and better lamp and called it the *sun*. The lamp is the real thing: the *sun* is but a tale, a children's story."

A World of "Nothing Buts"

If we swallow the psychological equivalent of this medicine, we find that like Alice we are growing smaller. Except that the world does not remain large and therefore wondrous. It shrinks too. For a world of "nothing buts" is a world of little interest. The secular psychological attitude leads us to the place where Lewis unhappily stood before his conversion: "Nearly all that I loved I believed to be imaginary, nearly all that I believed to be real I thought grim and meaningless."

So if the psychological version is the only reality, let us describe it truthfully. Let there be no talk of caring deeply and no palaver about fulfillment. The psychological society is dedicated to the proposition that there is no loyalty so strong it can't be scuttled and no desire so deep it can't be trivialized. We should be honest enough to talk about a dulling of experience instead of a heightening of experience, and to expose forthrightly the stifling of deep-seated passions. What is true of the psychotropic drugs is true, also, of the psychological ethos. Both tend to blunt our desires and our caring.

But there is an alternative. We could take another bit of psychological advice. That is, we could pay attention to our experience.

What does experience tell us? It tells us we are restless. Something in us simply won't come to terms. As soon as we secure the thing we thought would ease our desire, the old desire springs up again, still unfulfilled. None of the things the experts prescribe for quenching this yearning do the trick. Not even the much applauded discovery of self. We don't feel upon the encounter with self, "Ah! this is what I have been looking for all my life!" Any adult with an ounce of honesty knows all this.

In a backhanded way, even the behavioral scientists admit as much. Despite themselves, they are forced to pay homage to this infinite impulse. "With more comprehensive education," they will say, "with increasing knowledge and better understanding of social forces, we are coming to the point where we should be able to provide healthy, happy, and useful lives for all. The day is not far off when no need will have to go unsatisfied and no child will go unloved. . . ." And so on.

You have heard this kind of talk, I'm sure. There is no heaven, it says in effect, but this world can be made into a kind of heaven, once we learn to control the variables that affect happiness. To bribe us away from our sense of exile, we are assured that our present lodging can be fashioned into a suitable homeland after all. There is something in the whole situation that is reminiscent of Milton's fallen angels who, upon reaching the black and burning pit, try to convince one another that it isn't such a bad place after all.

The point is, it *is* a bad place. That is, it's a bad place if it's the only place. Because every instinct in us tells us this is not the place we were meant for. As a station on the way, as a temporary rest for weary travelers, we can accept it and even love it. But as the only place, as the final destination, it represents ultimate frustration. Make it as comfortable as you like, it will not do. Our instincts rebel.

The healthy mind works upwards not downwards. It sees a sun lamp and it thinks of the sun, not the other way around. We can, it's true, deny our instincts and work to eradicate them, and eventually we can be conditioned to believe that everything is less than it appears and that the substitute is preferable to the real thing. You can condition a child to prefer an orange-flavored powdered drink to orange juice. And a man can learn to prefer talks with his therapist to conversations with his friends. Some people do prefer sun lamps to the sun. Our nature can be corrupted so that we accept the lesser and forget the higher. And the more effectively this desensitization is carried out, the less likely its victims will have any awareness of what has happened. Those who have been well conditioned are no longer in a position to complain that something is missing. We may safely venture to say that many victims of secular psychology have already forgotten that there is an Overworld.

Remembering Where Home Is

To this point I have emphasized only natural instincts. They alone, of course, tell us that we were made for something more. But they can be easily drugged by the *thrum-thrum-thrum* of faddish concepts. That is where Christianity comes in. For it is very explicit about reminding us of our true homeland; where it is and how to get there.

That is why Christianity is full of reminders. "Remember the Sabbath day, to keep it holy." "Remember the word that I said to you." "Remember those who are in prison." "Do this in remembrance of me." "And now I want to remind you, my brothers, of the Good News which I preached to you." "Remember . . . what you were told in the past by the apostles of our Lord Jesus Christ." "Peter remembered . . . and he went out and wept bitterly." "In memory of His death and resurrection, we offer this bread." "Remember Christ our Saviour was born on Christmas Day." It is why Christians are asked to commit things to memory: prayers and commandments and hymns. *The Iliad* and *The Odyssey*, we are told, were most probably sung to their audiences because they were easier to remember that way. The rhythm and cadence of a poem or song is an aid to memory. For the same reason, Christians pray the psalms and sing hymns and follow a liturgical cycle that has a regular recurrence and read the Bible daily or try to.

Of course it's one of the things Christians are criticized for, even by other Christians: "Why can't they sing any new songs?"; "Church is always the same"; "I already know what I'm supposed to know." Yes, and you probably know that you should send your grandmother a thank-you note when she

gives you a present. But it's easy to forget. That's why
mothers and fathers and the people who care about us are
always reminding us of things: "Don't forget to thank your
grandmother"; "Remember to congratulate Johnny on his
new job"; "Remember to wear your motorcycle helmet." It
seems a bother. But without those reminders, we often
wouldn't remember.

Christianity won't let you forget. Christians are supposed
to pass on the story, to remind each other that they are on a
journey, and to make sure the next generation gets intact
the message and the map that goes with it. They are to sing
marching songs along the road to keep the spirits up and the
memory keen, and they must sing all the louder in the vicinity of Sirens or Circes.

Christians are not called on to create some new way of
salvation. It is not their business to engineer a better road or
to expand it to eight lanes or to redirect it to avoid swamps or
mountains or the hill of Golgotha. Their business is the
business of one foot up and one foot down.

The Unchanging Message

One of the main differences between the Christian message and the psychological one lies precisely here: the
Christian message does not change, while the psychological
one changes constantly. Psychologists are forever engaged
in building new roads, formulating new concepts, and carrying on more research. The explanation for this is partly
scientific curiosity and partly the humanitarian concern for
improving our lot—good things, of course. But could it also
be that this constant jockeying stems from a basic failure—
the failure to find a message that really satisfies? Why does
psychological insight never seem enough? Why do clients
keep showing up for booster shots of analysis as though there

were *one* insight they have missed? Could it be intended that all such efforts to make a personal or social utopia are doomed because this is not the right place for us to settle down?

Although Christians as individuals need improvement, they maintain without arrogance that the Christian message does not. It doesn't need to change because it satisfies as it is. Christians hold that they already have the truth that answers the inconsolable longing and that will eventually fill every need. The important thing for them is to remember faithfully.

The Hero of the Story

Of course appearances can be deceiving. On the surface, the secular world will often appear to hold more promise than the supernatural one. I confess with dismay that the churches sometimes allow dreariness to creep into their ritual. But the dreariness is not in the Bible. If one looks at Christ's life as depicted in the Gospels, one finds there something quite different from what we have been conditioned to believe is there by having read everything but the Gospels. Somehow the notion has gotten around that the New Testament is mainly a story about mercy and mildness: that Christ's mission was to teach peace, love, and brotherhood. But such a view is simply not supported by the Scriptures. True, the message of peace and brotherhood is there, but it is not the main message or the most repeated one. For one thing, the message of love and peace was not new to the ancient world. It could not be considered a gospel, since that word implies there is "news." For another thing, there is nothing in Christ's attitude about Himself to suggest that He saw Himself mainly as a teacher.

There is a strong suggestion that Jesus looked upon Himself as someone who had a job to do. And the quality of that task was not unlike the quest of a Greek or Roman hero. Those who are inclined to see in His life a parallel to other great teachers like Socrates or Buddha are, it strikes me, missing the point. Rather than come away with that impression, it would be more accurate if they would compare His life with the story of Aeneas or more precisely with the story of Odysseus. The final chapters of *The Odyssey* are among the most heart stirring in literature. Why? Because it is a romance of return after a long absence. The rightful king returns to his true homeland. He bides his time while he gathers a small band of family and retainers to his side, and then he strikes out against the false suitors to take back his land, his home, and his wife. It is noteworthy that Odysseus is not immediately recognized by his family; before he wins them he must first convince them by signs that he is in fact the true master, the true father, the true husband. This return is Odysseus' destiny, and every other piece of the adventure points to this climax.

In style the Gospels bear no similarity to mythology. They read like histories. But in substance they are closer to the heroic themes of *The Odyssey* and *The Aeneid* than to the philosophizing of Socrates or Plato or Aristotle or Buddha, or any of the other ancient teachers. Whether you believe the story or not, this is the way it must be read without breaking faith with the rules of commonsense textual analysis. What kind of story is it? An adventure story, an epic: a king returns to claim what is His. He hints that He is a bridegroom. He has a destiny: He must go up to Jerusalem to fulfill the prophecies; He must drink of a certain cup. All His wanderings are leading to a destined climax. But first He bides His time and gathers about Him a small group of believers who recognize the signs of His kingship. In order to restore the true homeland to His followers, He must heal an ancient cosmic breach. The price is His life—and He pays it.

What one encounters in the Gospels is a picture of a Man who knows quite clearly what He is about and what He must do and who will not be deterred from His course. He has come to win back what belongs to Him, and woe to the false suitors who would prevent His return. He has a strong destiny. And—audacity piled on reckless audacity —He wishes to sweep all others along with Him in this destiny.

The whole story is full of these things. An individual reading the Gospels for the first time without preconceptions for or against Christianity would not come away with the impression of a mild-mannered philosopher given to expressing His beliefs in carefully qualified opinions. To the contrary, the man seems as rash in His speech as in His actions. It is the language of heroes: sometimes crafty like Odysseus, sometimes bold like Achilles. He is given to calling people "fools" and "hypocrites." He indulges in fantastic metaphors about camels passing through a needle's eye. He makes inordinate boasts: "Destroy this temple, and in three days I will raise it up." He delivers stinging rebukes: "Are your minds so dull? You have eyes—can't you see? You have ears—can't you hear?" Above and beyond this He tells His followers that they do not belong to this world. He makes staggering promises to them of being lifted up, of glory, of mansions in another kingdom.

In this suggestion of something farther off and higher up, we find an echo of our experience of an inconsolable longing. It supports our suspicion that we are living by some mixup or mishap in an alien world, a place where, try as we may, we never quite feel at home. Deeper than our search for contentment, underneath our desire for self-fulfillment, a quiet but persistent voice whispers that someday we will have to fling our pack on our back and go off in search of our own country.

Two Basic Needs

These, of course, are high hopes. Too high, many would say. But whether or not the gospel promise is pie-in-the-sky, it is at any rate a pie, not a crust of stale stoicism. It is a pie that satisfies on two counts. First, it satisfies our need for reward. Second, it satisfies our need for a story.

It might be objected on the first count that the satisfaction of having done one's duty in life should be enough for the mature person without the bribe of stars and crowns. This strikes me as a noble sentiment, but a sentiment, nonetheless. It is a sentimental, not a realistic, view of the human condition; it assumes that we are all much more grown up than we really are—that we are in control, that we don't need attention, that we are already perfected. A truer account of our situation, I think, is given in André Malraux's *Anti-Memoirs:* one of his acquaintances, an old and experienced country priest, says, "There's no such thing as a grown-up person." The thrill at the idea of reaping a reward of approval from one you want very much to please may not be worthy of a stoic or of those psychologically minded persons who desire perfect self-sufficiency, but for most of us it fits a childlike and very human hope for recognition.

The New Testament satisfies a second need, the need for a story. And not just any story, but a romance that is also an adventure story.

Like all adventure stories, it contains certain elements. All adventure stories require the presence of good and evil and an eventual judgment against evil; all adventure stories require a quest or a journey; they all require that the hero or heroine pass various tests to save his or her life or save the day; and consequently all adventure stories contain an element of real danger. Many of the elements of Christianity that people find hard to stomach are the same elements that would be sorely missed if they were absent from an adventure or romance. Without the danger or the tests, the story would ring false. If in the fairy stories the evil prince and the blackguard stepuncle could sin with impunity, if the slain dragon counted for nothing as a test, if the prince could save the day by staying in his castle and studying philosophy, then nobody would read fairy stories. Suppose we read, "And if the stone is not returned to its proper place in the tower before the morning sun strikes the eastern wall, your kingdom and your bride are forfeit." Or suppose somebody in a story says, "Very well, I will give you three days. If you guess my name within that time, you may keep the child." What is the power and attraction of these conditions except that they are conditions—everything depends on them—and except that they impose a time limit? You do not have forever to choose and act, but your choice may affect your happiness forever after. The same sense of conditional happiness, of urgency, of monumental consequences runs through the Bible. "You may freely eat of every tree of the garden; but of the tree of the knowledge of good and evil you shall not eat, for in the day that you eat of it you shall die." "Before the cock crows twice, you will deny me three times." "The light is with you for a little longer. Walk while you have the light. . . ." In the Christian adventure everything depends not only on fulfilling the conditions but on acting now, without delay, lest the light should fade.

The Storytelling Instinct

The storytelling instinct, as I have suggested, is central to human psychology. We have an appetite for stories just as we have for food and drink. It is not a subtle and elusive need. It is quite plain. Yet psychologists have little to say about it except perhaps to suggest that Sleeping Beauty was afraid of sex. It's not just that psychology can't meet our need for a story. That part is understandable. What ought to concern us is the theft of all the elements that make interesting stories (and interesting lives) possible. To refuse strong attachments as Freud did or to deny evil as Rogers does or to reduce life to a reinforcement schedule as Skinner does is to sin against the soul of a story. It all suggests that a life is little more than a case study.

This psychological knack for cutting the core out of things should give us pause. When someone who professes to explain human nature and human behavior omits too many of the important details, the disinterested observer may be justified in wondering whether they are telling the whole story or, for that matter, whether the part that they are telling is at all credible.

Thomas Howard argues—and quite successfully I think—that the origin of fairy stories is not in our unconscious (as a psychologist might contend) but "in the Empyrean." All those stories about orphan boys who set out on a journey and remember faithfully what they were told by the old beggar woman, and battle temptation, and see through false disguises, and find at the end of their journey that they are not orphans at all but the son of the king—all those stories ring "bells in our imagination" because that, in fact, is The Story, "the only story there is, finally."[2]

Man is a storytelling animal. For this reason, as Tolkien suggested, God has given him a story to live. And, "There is no tale ever told that men would rather find was true . . . to reject it leads either to sadness or to wrath."[3] For to reject it means that (if we are honest) we must accept that we do live in the dismal kingdom, that our deepest hopes and desires will never come to fruition, and that no amount of progress will ever make up our loss.

Clearing Away the Fog

When you clear away the fog, those seem to be the choices. And although it is true, by-and-large, that people will follow their better natures when faced with a clear choice, clear choices are not abundant and jargon is. Faced with a choice between psychology, the modern-day stoicism, which seems to be telling us that we desire too much, and the Gospels, which seem to be saying that, if anything, we desire too little, it might be expected that our better natures would win out. Even our instincts for truth and beauty, however, can trip us up when half-truths wrap themselves up in the robes of expertise and pretend to be the givers of all good things.

Perhaps we ought to return, finally, to where we began. The young prince, the two children, and their companion, a Marsh-wiggle, have nearly abandoned both their better instincts and their memories to the cool and soothing rationality of the Underworld Queen. To prevent the enchantment from taking hold, the Marsh-wiggle, a simple but sound-minded creature, thrusts his foot into the fire:

"One word, Ma'am," he said, coming back from the fire, limping, because of the pain. "One word. All you've been saying is quite right, I shouldn't wonder. I'm a chap who always liked to know the worst and then put the best face I can on it. So I won't deny any of what you said. But there's one thing more to be said, even so. Suppose we *have* only dreamed, or made up, all those things—trees and grass and sun and moon and stars and Aslan himself. Suppose we have. Then all I can say is that, in that case, the made-up things seem a good deal more important than the real ones. Suppose this black pit of a kingdom of yours *is* the only world. Well, it strikes me as a pretty poor one. And that's a funny thing, when you come to think of it. We're just babies making up a game, if you're right. But four babies playing a game can make a play-world which licks your real world hollow. That's why I'm going to stand by the play world. I'm on Aslan's side even if there isn't any Aslan to lead it. I'm going to live as like a Narnian as I can even if there isn't any Narnia."

At this point the children, who are sinking under the stuporous effect of the queen's words, rally to the Marsh-wiggle's side and make their escape. Even children can tell a good story from a bad one.

CHAPTER 10

The Sacred and the Secular

When I was in college our history teachers told us that the most radical change in all history came with the advent of secularism. I only half understood. Twenty is not a good age for grasping the possibility that the world you grew up in might be deficient in crucial ways.

What they meant, of course, is that the world has lost its sense of the sacred. Every age but our own has recognized that the world is haunted by something uncanny and splendorous, something magical—something that requires sacred times, sacred places, and sacred ceremonies. Wherever the sacred seemed to reveal itself most strongly, people felt obliged to hallow those places: groves, springs, woodland clearings. Or sometimes upon those sites they would erect tents or temples or cathedrals.

Even in a secular world we may be visited with occasions of mysterious awe. It happens most often in natural surroundings, and a certain kind of stillness will bring it on. Upon an instant, nature seems under a gentle spell, the trees and sky standing in attendance on some other presence, waiting to do its bidding. Perhaps you are in a wood on a crisp autumn day and suddenly the leaves come rustling up from the forest floor, sweep along above it, and then begin swirling upwards around your head in golds and reds, carried there by an invisible breath of something in the air. You can account for it, and yet it seems unaccountable. At moments like this you can well understand why the ancients thought the trees were alive. You can still hear the murmuring of the dryads in the rustle of the leaves. Or at night, far out in the country, you look up at the celestial vault and realize, as you cannot in the city, its vastness and beauty. If you are normal you cannot help but feel a certain insignificance in yourself and at the same time a certain gratitude.

What we feel at such times is what Peter and the other apostles felt on the Mount of Transfiguration: "It is good for us to be here." And like them we feel we must respond in some appropriate way. Peter wanted to erect three tents. We might feel that silence is appropriate, or if we talk, our tone is likely to be hushed and reverential, the very tenor of our conversation changed. We become, in short, aware of a different atmosphere or aspect in the world. When we say that we live in a secular world, we mean that in other ages people lived in that sacred atmosphere much more than we do. Another way of putting it would be to say that for them the world was suffused with an extraordinary importance, for at any ordinary point of place or time the sacred world might break in upon the everyday one.

God's Awesomeness

But that is not quite all that needs to be said. It is one thing to have an uncanny sense of God's sacred presence at night or in the forest. It is another thing altogether when that dread Presence manifests itself directly. Moses, Isaiah, and Jeremiah were about as brave as men could be, yet in the presence of the Almighty they shrank back like terrified children. Even then, what they saw was only the veiled Presence. No one could look upon God's face and live.

You get the same sense of terror in the reaction of the apostles when Jesus calmed the waves. They were very much afraid, more afraid of Him than of the swelling sea. "What kind of man is this?" they asked. What must it be like to realize suddenly that the man next to you in the boat might come from beyond the stars? We can suppose the experience might be similar to that moment in a well-made science fiction film when the characters come face to face with a being utterly unlike themselves.

But with a difference. For in that moment of recognition—that moment, for example, when Peter pleads with the Lord to depart from him—we realize that we are the creatures with the bulging eyes and reptilian skin.

It is a profound mistake to forget the total otherness of God or to imagine that an encounter with Him would be anything less than traumatic. Even without revelation, men have always sensed this. They felt that the universe contained a great power or, rather, that a great Power contained the universe and presided over it. And under that Power a man took care what he said and did.

The Loss of the Sacred

All this bespeaks a spirit that has been lost or debased today. But to say the present age has lost the sense of the sacred is not to say it has forgotten all about God, because even a thoroughgoing secularist may retain a vague belief. It means, rather, to have forgotten who God is, His overwhelming nature. The secular mind does not always find it necessary to deny God, but it must always reduce Him to a comfortable size. Above all else He must be a manageable God who does not watch or judge.

For example, a recent popular film depicts God as a cigar-smoking older man whose agenda for the human race contains nothing that would be offensive to a reader of *The New York Times*. Another popular film is a parody of the life of Christ. A current off-Broadway play makes fun of the crucifixion. It would be easy to label these as blasphemous, yet one gets the impression that the filmmakers (the play is another matter) are scarcely aware that a category such as blasphemy exists. To be a blasphemer in the true sense of the word you first have to recognize that some things are holy. And there is no sense expecting the makers of these films to understand absolute holiness when they have not yet grasped simple concepts such as good and bad or proper and improper.

What is especially shocking about these entertainments is that they are so casually accepted by the public. One would think that God had become a tame animal to be taken out and put on display for our amusement. A dangerous attitude, that. One thinks of the tourists to Yellowstone Park each year who get mauled because they fail to heed the signs instructing them that the bears are *not* tame.

Understanding the Sacred

To the secular mind nothing is mysterious, nothing is awesome, nothing is beyond commercialization. But it is one thing to say all this, and another to realize how it came to pass. To understand why we have lost the sense of the sacred, we need to understand more about sacred realities.

1. The sacred reality is the absolute reality around which the rest of life is oriented. Without it, there could be no fixed point of reference for deciding higher or lower, better or worse. Without it, everything would be relative. Everything would sink into a bland homogeneity. This experience would mean no more than that experience, this place no more than that, this day no more than the last one. Without the sacred, you have a state of complete and desolate equality in which nothing special exists.

To get the point, imagine a city built around a central square with some magnificent public building at its heart. Now picture boulevards radiating outward from that point, with smaller squares or circles along them. The houses in the city will be of various sizes and architecture, but each will have some relation to the park or circle nearest it and also to the central square. You may not live in the best house, but there will always be something special about it if only because it bears a relation to special places. Then imagine a city with no central place, only block upon block of identical buildings: each block the same size, each building and dwelling the same size and design, the whole thing stretching out for mile after square mile.

Which would you prefer to live in? If you choose the first, you will understand the attitude our ancestors took, for that is the kind of universe they preferred to live in.

2. Reality exists in a hierarchy. "According to this conception," wrote Lewis in his *Preface to Paradise Lost,* "degrees of value are objectively present in the universe. Everything except God has some natural superior; everything except unformed matter has some natural inferior. The goodness, happiness, and dignity of every being consists in obeying its natural superior and in ruling its natural inferiors." We might add: "within their proper spheres." One properly feels awe at the music of a Beethoven. But a Beethoven must still obey the police. Under the law he stands no higher than the town drunk. What we are not allowed to do, however, is to say that the drunk who bangs on the piano keys is making music as good as Beethoven's. All things are not equal.

All things, however, take their value from the fact that they are related to the best thing, which is God. To worship God is simply to be in touch with reality, to see things as they are. Likewise, to see meaning in the things about us is to have some recognition of the place that they take in God's hierarchy. This does not mean that God is in everything in a pantheist sense—that would rule out hierarchy. It means, rather, that all things point to their Creator if we look at them rightly.

3. Everyday things take their meaning insofar as they correspond to sacred things. In ages past, this was taken for granted. The authority of a father over his children derived from the fact that there is a Father who rules over all. Civil order was, ideally, a reflection of heavenly order.

In fact, all things were thought to be connected. And for this reason, ordinary life was full of meaning. The passage of seasons was a reminder of the passage of a man's life. The coming of spring was a reminder that there is always new life. Ploughing and seeding and fruitfulness were reminders of men and women bringing children into the world. A girl cutting her hair might find her thoughts drifting to a young man cutting wheat in a field. And the thoughts of a man cutting wheat in a field might turn to thoughts of a girl cutting her hair. It was a poetic way of looking at things: everything was metaphor; everything meant more than itself. Connections and correspondences ran in all directions. A caterpillar in its shroud or a seed buried in the ground hinted at some greater metamorphosis for all those willing to die to self.

But we must not suppose that in these ages people were incapable of understanding the modern view. They understood it well enough to know that it was not worth living for. The modern view is expressed, of course, in Shakespeare's, "Tomorrow, and tomorrow, and tomorrow, creeps in this petty pace. . . ." If, when you boil things down, this means nothing and that means nothing, life loses its significance, time becomes a meaningless repetition of days. But if *this* everyday thing is a clue to *that* greater rhythm in the universe, the struggle may indeed be worth it.

4. The sacred is set apart. It gives meaning to everyday life, but it is not the same as everyday life. Consequently, holy things are not available for everyday use. You don't lease out a church on weekdays to local retailers. And sacred ceremonies require special behavior. You don't wear a T-shirt to a church wedding. The church is not the street. The sacred grove is not the marketplace. The sacramental wine is not for the evening cocktail party. What is sacred is extraordinarily special, and whatever attaches to it is lifted out of the ordinary.

When the sacred is cheapened everything is cheapened. This can happen anytime something is set apart for an exclusive use. Let us say that you have received a family heirloom: a ring from your mother or a pocket watch from your father. It is meant as a special gift for your use. It is a privilege and also, in a sense, a duty entrusted. You do not go off with it to the nearest pawn shop just because you happen to be hard up for cash. To do such a thing, even under dire straits, makes us feel cheap. It is not only the gift that has been devalued; the quality of all things seems diminished when we act that way.

5. The sacred requires ceremony. This follows from the previous point. Because the sacred is not ordinary, we will not want to approach it in an ordinary way. Our response should be special. Just as Moses had to remove his sandals before walking on the holy ground, we feel it proper to make gestures that acknowledge awe and reverence. We wear our best clothes, we move with dignity, we sing special hymns, we pray and petition.

This is our natural inclination anyway. The things we love to do, the things we consider important, are things we want to do ceremonially. We make preparations for them, we take time with them. We turn our family meals into ceremonies when they could be arranged much more pragmatically.

When we give a present we wait for the right place and moment. We make a minor ceremony out of it. We have rituals of wrapping and unwrapping, writing cards and reading them. We surround graduations with pomp and flourish. There are entrance marches and recessionals, gowns and tassels, scrolls of paper and ritual applause. The whole thing could be accomplished more efficiently with computerized mailings. But a deep instinct tells us to do otherwise.

6. Obedience is the key to it all. Lewis has argued that the festivity and panoply of earthly celebrations are hints of the Great Dance—his image of heaven. The joy of heaven, in this view, can be best imagined in terms of the solemn, measured joyfulness of a dance in which each takes his part, and each has his turn, and where all are obedient to the deep pattern of the dance. It is like that, of course, with ordinary folk dancing or line dancing. The freedom and frolic of the dance depend on obedience to the rules of the dance, to the pattern of rising and falling, retreat and advance, deference and courtesy. The reward of the dance, then, comes to those who are willing to submit themselves to learning the steps. Lewis went so far as to suggest that an unceremonious approach to life was a species of pride. "The modern habit of doing ceremonial things unceremoniously is no proof of humility," he wrote, "rather it proves the offender's inability to forget himself in the rite. . . ."[1]

Psychology and the Sacred

With that point we can return to the present situation. You can see, of course, that in laying out the elements that mark the sacred sense of life, we have charted a collision course with the psychological society. No frame of mind could be better constructed to resist the sacred than the one we are encouraged in today. Think of a youngster surrounded by wealth, waited on by servants, catered to and indulged—a spoiled little master. Put him in a normal home where everyone is expected to pitch in, and he will not only be unable to accept it, he will hardly comprehend it. He has no psychological preparation for it. That child's situation is like our own. We are psychologically ill-prepared to recognize or accept the demands of the sacred realm. The proper conditions are absent. Assertiveness, self-attention, and the like are not the kind of practice we need for taking our place in the Dance.

Three Habits of Mind

There are three psychological habits of mind, in particular, that interfere with our ability to appreciate the sacred. I have already mentioned them in other contexts: they are subjectivism, reductionism, and naturalism. The three overlap, but let us see if we can tease them apart in order to look at their effects.

Subjectivism

The person who has allowed himself to lapse into a subjectivist frame of mind believes that no idea or object is of any more value than any other idea or object. If you get to arguing with him, you quickly find that he has no idea of higher or lower, better or worse. He is set on the equality of all ideas and will give equal weight to the word of God and the opinions of rock stars.

One other thing he can't grasp is the idea of specialness. In his mind everything reduces to the same level. It is not unusual to meet people who in the course of a conversation will traverse topics ranging from shopping and taxes to incest and oral sex without batting an eyelash or changing their tone of voice. Nor will the presence of children or teen-agers have any effect on what they say. Along with the ability to discriminate one topic from another they have lost the ability to discriminate between conversation appropriate for adults and conversation appropriate for youth.

Long-term psychotherapy will sometimes have this effect on individuals. Television has that effect on the entire culture. Anything and everything is considered fair game for presentation. Nothing is held back from public view or public discussion because nothing is thought to have any special standing. If anyone complains about this state of affairs, he will be told that nowadays we are more honest or that all points of view must be presented. But, of course, it has nothing to do with honesty, and a great deal to do with profits. Profit, however, is not the whole explanation. Men have always been greedy, but most men in most ages have understood that some things are in a different sphere of value. This generation does not.

You can find no better example of this frame of mind than the attempt to "make Sunday like every other day." That is the wording on a piece of legislation currently being debated in my state. My state happens to be one of the holdouts. Sundays are already less special and more like other days than was the case a few years ago. You have only to think of Sunday "best," Sunday meals, Sunday picnics, Sunday visits, and other Sunday rituals as they were practiced only a short while ago to see the change. There are always those who will want to open up Sunday to business as usual, and without a sense of the sacred there is little rationale for resisting them. It will be done in the name of convenience, of course—a public service. But in a hundred subtle ways the attitude filters down and affects us all. Sunday becomes no different from Saturday or any other workless day. Its special quality and tone will begin to disappear. This is because the special quality of Sunday does not lie in the fact that it is a day of leisure but in the fact that it is part of a sacred cycle.

To see this you need only think of the many people with leisure time on their hands who still take no pleasure in life. An endless succession of leisure days with nothing to mark them off or give them significance can become as meaningless as the drudgery of endless work days. But the sacred vision allows us to see that the repetition of days is not a repetition but a rhythm—like the rhythm of a march. It means we are getting somewhere, not just marking time.

Reductionism

Here we come back to the traditional belief that it is the sacred things that give meaning to the rest of life. The effect of suppressing the sacred vision has not been to make life more sunny and rational but to make it more absurd. Recall for a moment what we said earlier about the psychologist's habit of reductionism, the habit of saying "this is nothing but this." Think of behaviorism, which tells us that all behavior, no matter how worthy it may appear, is nothing but a chain of conditioned responses. Or Freudian psychology, which claims that we are nothing but a system of psychic pumps, valves, and drains. Or physiological psychology, which says that behavior is nothing but electrical impulses leaping across synapses.

Notice that in all cases the *this* we end up with seems considerably less than the *this* we started off with. Psychological thinking is reductionist in the full sense of the word. It reduces or makes smaller. It is always in the business of ripping the curtain aside so that we may see that the Wizard is only a little man. This approach amounts to saying that there is nothing behind things, or very little. It is the exact opposite of that other habit of mind that runs upward toward the sacred, seeing images of the greater in the lesser and tending toward the enlargement of all things.

The old view, as I have said, is a poetic one. But that does not mean "removed from reality." It can be argued that poetry is very close to reality. We moderns freely admit that we have become alienated from nature, from ourselves, from the work of our hands. Yet, if we look back to a time when people were still in touch with these things, we find that they expressed themselves poetically as a matter of course. *The Iliad, The Odyssey,* and *Beowulf* were poetry put to song because song and poetry were thought to lie close to the heart of things. The old expression, "there's no rhyme or reason to it," suggests that the two were once thought to be connected. There is something reasonable about rhyme: it provides recognition and resolution, anticipation and reward, regular recurrence—all of which seem to respond to or complement some reality in us as well as some reality in the world. The best stories for young children, for example, always have a boisterous refrain such as "little pigs, little pigs, let me come *in*," and children respond by asking to hear them again and again. Adults have a similar need. A work song, for instance, will give both rhyme and reason to what otherwise seems a dull, repetitive task. In short, rhyme seems to answer to some deeper reason in the Universe.

There is some mystery here, to be sure. But we make a mistake to equate mysterious with meaningless. On the contrary, it is the removal of mystery and metaphor that quite often leads to the conviction that the world makes no sense. Psychological reductionism, which by its nature is opposed to mystery, not only takes the poetry out of life but the rationale as well. While trying to make sense of life, it takes away the sense that life has any meaning. You can see how this works if you have tried to explain some natural phenomenon to a child in terms that were too naturalistic only to have him immediately lose interest. "If that is all there is to it," he seems to be saying, "let's drop the subject."

An instance of misguided reductionism can be found in the primers used in grammar schools. They are usually written by committee, by men and women who are working not from any larger vision but from narrow pedagogical theories (often psychological in nature). The object of these is to reduce language to its simplest components but the result is often to strip off anything of excitement and power. A child who reads, "Nan had a pad. Nan had a tan pad. Dad ran. Dad ran to the pad," can be forgiven if the idea of reading does not appeal to him. The most recent vocal critic of this reductionism is himself a psychologist—Bruno Bettelheim. Bettelheim is quite right in saying that the poor reading skills of children can be traced to the meaningless texts they are given. "Nan had a tan pad" has rhyme but it has no rhythm; that is, there is nothing poetic about it. It can't match "little pigs, little pigs." I think the ordinary reaction of children to these new books (boredom) is proof that once you squeeze out that type of rhyme you have squeezed out the reason, too.

The "this is nothing but that" approach has a further consequence. When that climate of thought prevails, there is no point setting anything apart as special; although, as we have seen, this setting apart is the very essence of the sacred. When you have torn down hierarchy and reduced everything to its lowest common denominator, there is precious little room for appreciating sacred things.

Now if the sacred order is the true one, this way of thinking will get us in a muddle. Once again, our modern approaches to schooling provide an example. It is no secret that public schools are rife with vandalism and violence, that they harbor youngsters who respect neither learning nor their teachers. Part of the reason, I think, is that the schools have lost their status as special places, places set apart. Now schools may not be holy places, but it is proper to place them above profane life. That has always, until recently, been the consensus. Expressions such as "hallowed halls," "temple of learning" and "groves of academe" are reminders of that attitude. The school, as one educator recently put it, "is not an extension of the street, the movie theater, a rock concert, or a playground."

I find the quote of special interest, because it comes from a man who fifteen years earlier had helped pioneer the effort to blend school and street, an effort that he now suggests had the result not of elevating students but of reducing the schools to the level of the things around them. Schools, he now says, should be special places with special requirements such as dress codes because "the way one dresses is an indication of an attitude toward a situation. And the way one is *expected* to dress indicates what that attitude ought to be." Such symbols, he observes, not only reflect feelings but create them just as "kneeling in church, for example, reflects a sense of reverence but also engenders reverence."[2]

This author, Neil Postman, has most recently written about the disappearance of childhood. He says, and I think there can be little doubt he is correct, that the distinctions and dividing lines between children and adults have largely vanished. We are used to speaking glibly about social change, but this is a change of the first magnitude. Quite suddenly, children are talking and behaving in ways that would have been considered improper for adults only a short time ago. Adult sexual behavior? Yes, but along with that, adult cynicism and adult crime and adult depression, alcoholism, and suicide. By and large, Postman blames television for this development, but he makes it clear that television has this effect because it destroys notions of mystery, hierarchy, and sacredness.

Naturalism

These things, of course, can only be preserved where there is an understanding of roles and the behavior proper to one's role. And this leads us to the third habit of mind encouraged by psychology: the emphasis on spontaneity or naturalism. The word *naturalism* sometimes refers to a philosophic system, but here I mean it as behavior based on impulse or desire alone. Psychological naturalism tends to blame the socialization process for most of our ills. This emphasis involves a corresponding distrust of social roles.

Now I am well aware that role playing can sometimes lead to artificiality. But to read the literature of popular psychology, you would think this is all that happens: that playing roles only means being dishonest or fake. This is a new idea and is foreign to most other ages and cultures. Even among the most primitive people the idea is not accepted. Men and women in tribal societies do not seek to be "natural" but to play their roles well. Proper behavior in regard to one's position—whether one of command or of deference or of equality—is what makes the man, not nature.

In fact, roles are indispensable. We have only to consider what life would be like without them to see this. What kind of society would it be where teachers refused to teach and policemen refused to enforce the law? There are people, some prominent psychologists among them, who would welcome such a world. But I think most of us would find it a cause for considerable worry. We are rightly concerned when the authority of a role is abused, but we are equally shocked when legitimate roles are not respected. Almost everyone, for instance, is appalled to see a family where an obnoxious child orders his parents about. Even the thought of equality in families—the idea, as Lewis put it, that one's mother is "simply a fellow citizen"—is disconcerting. Now, it seems to me that all these ideas we have about roles and authority are connected to the idea of hierarchy and, from thence, to the sacred. It follows that a complete secularization is a formula for much confusion about roles: the kind of confusion that results in teachers or parents reducing their role with children to friend or equal. In this context, even a simple code such as respecting elders or honoring one's parents will be hard to grasp. The framework that made sense out of the code has been lost.

Now let us take a step further. I believe that if you check your experience you will find that roles are not only necessary but liberating. They allow us to accomplish things we might not be able to accomplish were we to rely on our moods alone. The policeman or soldier's role, for instance, helps him to overcome his natural fear and frees him to act more bravely than he might as a private citizen. The parade leader in his costume is allowed to swagger, strut, and somersault his way down the street, something he is not as free to do on his walk to the office. The roles required of us at a ceremony or celebration allow us to be festive or gracious even when our natural mood might not be equal to the occasion.

It's true, of course, that from time to time we all fall down in our roles. Keeping them up is no easy thing. But the response to this difficulty is not to call for their disposal. Roles were instituted in the first place because they were seen as the best way to protect freedom from arbitrary force. People found out soon enough where a purely "natural" instinctualism led. Please notice I have put "natural" in quotes; it seems to me that a true naturalness will be reflected in a humble willingness to accept our place in the sacred hierarchy. That, in any event, is the Christian view. God created our natures, and He created them in such a way that they would only reach their fullness by a supernatural completion. The difference between that view and the modern one is the difference between seeing life as hollow and seeing it as an enchanted hollow.

Two Cities

But I suppose it is an almost impossible task to tell a secular society that its only hope of bliss lies in the one thing it is most opposed to. I have tried to show that our own specialness depends on our relation to the absolute specialness of God and that a world emptied of holiness is a world emptied of meaning. But it is difficult to convince the citizen of the secular city of this when all he sees about him works to convince him that there is no plan and no specialness, only grim repetition.

From ground level that is often the way cities do appear. But if you have ever been in a plane at night looking down on a great metropolitan area and seen the cities and towns connected like a vast network of jewels, you cannot escape the impression that there is, after all, some meaning and purpose to it. Indeed a very beautiful purpose.

That experience, if we have had it, should remind us there are quite different ways of looking at cities. And, for that matter, there are quite different ways of looking at all things. Even now, by the report of apostles and saints, we are part of a vast jeweled network called the City of God.

CHAPTER 11

The American Spirit

I hope the last chapter hasn't left you with the impression that psychology is the only barrier between us and the sacred sense of things. There are certain elements in the American spirit that work against it, too.

In fact, much of present-day psychology takes its character from the American spirit. Think of a rather staid and formal European who immigrates to these shores and gradually adopts our more relaxed habits and casual attitudes. Something like that happened with psychology. Once it moved from Europe to America it adopted a spirit of autonomy and equality.

The point is, many of the attitudes you find in psychology are simply American attitudes. I remember reading a passage from Dr. Carl Rogers's biography and being struck by the sheer Americanism of it. It is from a letter of resignation to the counseling staff at the University of Wisconsin: "What a large streak of pioneering spirit there is in me. I really am kin to the old frontiersman, and my feeling at the present time is that I can hardly wait to throw my pack on my back and leave the settlement behind. I itch to get going! . . . The thought of new wilderness to explore . . . is like wine in my blood. . . ."[1]

This is really no different from Walt Whitman's "Song of the Open Road," written a hundred years or so before, or from the attitude of the original pioneers. And when you think of the ideas pioneered by Rogers, doesn't it look as though he's simply taken the frontier spirit and applied it to the self? You encounter in his psychology the same impatience with society and settled ways as you would in any leather-jerkined mountain man going west. Whenever I read Dr. Rogers or some like-minded psychologist, my mind conjures up visions of hardy individuals breaking trails through unmapped regions of the self: personality pioneers in search of limitless inner possibilities. Read Rogers, and you will see what I mean. This promise that the frontier is still open is the promise underlying much of popular psychology and accounts in no small part for its popularity.

The American Spirit

There is nothing terribly radical, then, about contemporary American psychology. You will find similar sentiments all through American history, which is why it should be no surprise that the American spirit is not always in harmony with the sacred one. Notions of hierarchy and submission will not.go down well with people who wrested their freedom from a monarchy. The first Americans were fond of saying "We have no king here!" or "Don't tread on me!" or "One man's as good as another."

That attitude prevails to this day. Equality is still the main plank in our platform. You can see there's not much room for an idea like "degrees of value . . . objectively present in the universe" to slip in.

These ideas and attitudes have been double-edged. They have been good for us in a hundred ways that need no explanation here, and yet at the same time they can come between us and an appreciation of the wonder of those things that are not in the realm of written constitutions and voting booths. A man too thoroughly imbued with the American spirit or the spirit of psychology is like a man who brings a radio into the woods. He won't notice the subtle sounds of leaves whispering over his head or brooks muttering at his feet. The sound he carries with him blocks it all out. He has violated the condition for appreciating the strangeness and otherness of nature. The same point applies to the man who carries about with him inflated ideas about equality; he does not have the right spirit for apprehending the sacred and so, when it comes near, he won't notice it.

The Americanization of Christianity

Now a step further—and I fear it is a step onto thin ice. Or into a bramble thicket. But it is the step that logically follows. It is this: just as Christianity is sometimes strongly influenced by psychology, so also it is affected by the American spirit. This was the thesis of a now classic book published in the mid-fifties under the title, *Protestant, Catholic, Jew.* The author, Will Herberg, observed that the three major denominations in America, whatever their differences with each other, all took on a distinctly American character. In the process of adapting to the American Way, Christians and Jews also learned to accommodate their faith to it.

In other words, if you were a Methodist or a Catholic or a Jew and you found a discrepancy or conflict between your religious faith and your faith in the American vision, the tendency would be for you to downplay those elements of your belief that didn't fit and to emphasize those that did. You wouldn't do this consciously, but there would be a strong pull in that direction. After decades and decades of assimilation, your faith might have a decidedly democratic tone to it. It would have something of the independent American spirit about it and something of the optimistic

American faith in positive thinking, and it might even have some of the spirit of American enterprise about it.

A Needed Balance: Form and Faith

You can easily see, then, how an American Christian would be attracted to churches that downplay formality and structure in favor of spontaneity and equality. This is not simply a Protestant phenomenon. You will find Catholics who want to celebrate mass informally around a kitchen table or who hold charismatic prayer meetings that rival any pentecostal church for unstructured spontaneity. Naturally we won't want to look at these phenomena in purely sociological terms and conclude that it's all the influence of the American spirit. That would not be giving much credit to the influence of the Holy Spirit. What I want to talk about, rather, is the balance that a Christian must maintain.

One of the constant temptations to all Christian churches is to lapse into dry formalism, and therefore one of the constant requirements of the Christian life is to pay attention to the promptings of God's Spirit—but remembering all the time that it is almighty God we worship and not presuming to become too casual about the way we approach Him. You have to be continually resisting temptations to conventionalism and yet never for a moment let yourself believe that God is the sort of being you may walk up to with an air of unbuttoned egalitarianism. Each age and society has its own dangers, however, and formalism does not seem to be the immediate threat to ours. The danger, as I see it, is that if we are not careful we shall drift more and more in the direction of a feet-on-the-table attitude about God, as though we were sitting around with Him in a heavenly mansion trading stories about life on Earth. It is possible, in short, even for Christians to lose the idea of the sacred.

We mustn't think that because we are Christians we have absolute immunity to the trends of the day. The fact of the matter is, Christians often fall prey to the same three habits of mind that render the psychological society as a whole incapable of appreciating the sacredness of God and His creation. How do they apply to Christians?

Christian Reductionism

Let's consider reductionism first. God did not create a simple world, and He has not given us a simple religion. The doctrine of the Incarnation is every bit as subtle as the doctrine of protons and electrons, and much more so. Most Christians realize this and try to keep the whole faith intact with all the difficult and mysterious parts and all the stumbling blocks, because what we have been given is, after all, the sacred Word of God, which is to be passed on as it was given to us. Still, you will come across some Christians who want to boil it down to a few formulas as though the way of faith were a simple thing like a recipe for apple turnover. You find ministers of the Word who have reduced the gospel message to the social gospel, or to the gospel of success, or to the gospel of positive thinking, or who have reduced Christ to the level of a good business partner.

There is even a danger here of concentrating too much on Christ as our friend. It is true that Christ is our brother and our friend, but it is a fact that ought to fill us with reticence and shyness; and we make a mistake to think He is nothing more than that. If He is just a friend, after all, He is in no position to save us. Of course, it is much more *comfortable* to think of Christ as our friend. You will see, however, that once a person confines Christ to that role alone, he can quickly lose sight of Christ's transcendent glory. He begins to have an attitude toward Christ that some people have toward celebrities they believe they have an "in" with. Most of us are familiar with people who are in the habit of saying things like "the Lord spoke to me and told me to do this," or "the Lord wants you to do that." The ordinary reaction to this is to feel a bit irked. Who do they think God is anyway? How did they come to be on terms of such easy familiarity with Him? Do they think they have Him in their pocket? Yes, by all means a personal relationship with Jesus. But let us have a little humility about it, and let us not trivialize that idea by reducing "personal" to what the world means by it. I think it is helpful whenever we are tempted to reduce God to a level slightly above our own to remind ourselves of the question asked of Job when he presumed to debate with the Almighty: "Where were you when I laid the foundations of the earth?" Job, who realized he wasn't anywhere in the vicinity at the time, wisely kept silent after that.

Christian Subjectivism

A second habit we considered last chapter was subjectivism. Our criticism of psychology was directed at the habit of thinking that says "I can believe anything I want." As Christians, we ought to take care that we don't end up with a similar attitude that says "Nobody tells me what to believe except the Holy Spirit." There are some Christians who are really more concerned with guarding their personal autonomy than in listening to the Holy Spirit. Or, to put it another way, sometimes Christians confuse the Holy Spirit with the American spirit; that is, they think religion, too, is a matter of equality and democracy and of hitting the trail in search of a new experience whenever the spirit moves them.

Experience is really the key word here. For some Christians it has a higher standing than Scripture. The reason, I think, is that in our society one's personal experience is beyond criticism or judgment. If I say I've experienced true enlightenment, who are you to say I haven't? It seems somehow undemocratic to question the validity of another person's inner feelings. Yet, when we rely on this criterion alone, we run the danger of making our faith a purely subjective phenomenon. You can see, I trust, the parallel with secular thinking: there are persons who will swear by encounter groups or meditation or drugs because of the powerful experience these things have provided them. And there is, of course, no way to gainsay them. They will simply fall back on their experience. They know it's true, and that's that.

But you will notice also in such natures that this attitude is usually accompanied by another that claims a sort of charismatic authority to transcend ordinary human paths. Not for them the slow step-by-step progress of pilgrims. If they can find a shortcut to the holy mountain or steal a foretaste of heavenly food, be sure they will take it and think it only their due.

The type of person I refer to thinks he is entitled to lap up as much experience as he can. For some, that becomes the sole aim of life. They collect experiences the way others collect antiques. Christians are not as prone to that temptation, but it is still a temptation. And the response to it is to recall that our Lord's words were "If you love me, you will keep my commandments," not "If you love me, you will have wonderful inner experiences."

Now, if you have an intense experience of the presence of God in your life, I don't say it is anything else *than* the presence of God. But if you find yourself trying to manufacture these experiences or if you come to the point where you think the ordinary means of approaching God are not worth your time, then that is the point for taking stock. If you find yourself continually experimenting with this kind of ex-

traordinary piety or that kind of unique religious phenomenon, you need to ask some questions of yourself. The ex-
perimental spirit is fine for many things, but if we are to take
our place in a great sacred dance we will want to get the
basic steps down before we think of improvising solos.

Our attitude here has to be a long-range one. Saint Paul
reckoned that "the sufferings of this present time are not
worth comparing with the glory that is to be revealed to us."
And I think the same can be said about our present feelings
of religious exhilaration. There is something far beyond that
in store for us. But I rather think the way to get to it is the
way of humble reverence and worship, not the way of striving after emotional experience.

Christians and Spontaneity

This brings us to the third habit of mind, the distrust of
roles and the corresponding stress on spontaneity. Many
psychologists, as we have noted, disparage role playing, but
then so do many Christians. There has always been a non-
conformist spirit within some branches of Christianity. The
admirable face of it shows itself in a refusal to conform to
worldly values. But it has also often meant simply a refusal of
all forms or formalities. The most common "form" that this
informal attitude takes is the unstructured prayer meeting
and the impromptu prayer. You may even encounter some
Christians who won't use the Lord's Prayer because it's too
formal, and you will certainly come across many who will
never say grace the same way twice because of the high
value they put on spontaneity.

Because spontaneous emotions arise without apparent ex-
ternal cause, they are valued as evidence of the working of
the Spirit. No doubt that is often true. The point I would like
to make, however, is that this is another case where Chris-

tian values suspiciously coincide with cultural ones. Not that you couldn't find Christian sects in Europe that practiced nonconformity and spontaneous expressions of fervor. You could, both before and after the Reformation. In America, however, this kind of Christianity became more widespread. The dictionary gives, as one definition of spontaneity, "unconstrained and unstudied in manner or behavior"—almost a definition of the American character. It fits with our image of ourselves as "just plain folks." Now that attitude is fine for neighbors chatting over the back fence or even for a New England town meeting: we have no king here, after all. But we mustn't let that color our whole outlook because we *do* have a King in heaven, and we must ask if that is the proper attitude with which to approach Him.

Spontaneity and Specialness

Once again, as you see, I am back to the subject of the sacred, and I am back to the more specific point that egalitarian and informal habits of mind can subvert the sacred sense. I wish here to consider two points.

First is the danger of losing the idea that the sacred is special and set apart. Catholics and high church Protestants are often criticized for the use of vestments, candles, and elaborate gestures. But how else should we indicate the specialness of God's presence? It is quite true that God can get along without these aids to devotion. But can we? Part of the purpose of ceremony is to remind us that we are in the presence of extraordinary mysteries. The life of the church is not everyday life: it isn't business as usual. It is the sacred world not the profane one. Doesn't it make sense, therefore, to keep it distinct from the profane world? Should a minister or priest, for example, wear street clothes in church? If you will allow that, would you want him to wear

[169]

Bermuda shorts? If not, why not? Isn't it a matter of the specialness and solemnity of his calling that demands a certain formality? I am not about to enter into a theological debate here about the priesthood of all believers. I merely want to call attention to the dangers of supposing that the worship of God is no different from any other activity. Because, if it is not, why make *any* fuss over it?

The second point is connected to the first. As we know, the spontaneous approach to worship often comes down to emotionalism, sometimes, it seems, to a mere show of emotion. This is certainly the very opposite of a kind of haughty formalism you find in some churches. And yet isn't it, in its own way, a form of self-absorption? Instead of forgetting ourselves in the rite, isn't it at times, a way of putting ourselves right into the center of attention?

It is an unfortunate fact that for some people worship service is primarily a vehicle for personal expressions and displays of individuality—the sort of things we might be tempted to criticize if we found them in a secular encounter group. If we are inclined to defend this as a more authentic worship, we should remember that "authenticity" is also a catchword of the encounter philosophy. We need to consider here what authentic really means.

Is a person most authentic when he is having a burst of emotion? When he is drunk and expressing himself freely and copiously? Isn't it rather the case that when we think of a friend's or relative's essential attributes, we think of his reliable, habitual, deep-grained responses rather than those surface parts of his personality that are subject to sudden crying or sudden volubility? In like manner God is more interested in the underlying character a person brings to worship than in his emotional state of the moment. And, therefore, shouldn't we be striving toward a form of worship that is also faithful and reliable and not subject to the fluctuating moods of the individual? What Christ has done for us, and not what we do for Him, needs to take center stage.

Sometimes prayer meetings or sacred rituals will have a powerful emotional effect, but if this becomes the chief thing for us, we will have missed the main point. The sacred must have an objective and special character that is independent of our ability to rouse ourselves or of the pastor's ability to be creative. We are not in heaven yet, and we do not have the vision of God's face ever before us like the angels. We still need all the help in worshiping Him we can get. It is this way with all the most important human activities. We are foolish to try to handle them with our own emotional resources alone. We wisely hand over to custom and ceremony the task of helping us through marriages, funerals, and other important moments, not because we are cold formalists but because we are only humans who stand in the face of great mysteries.

Wagon Wheels and Worship

If all of this sounds too high blown (or too high church) consider a practical matter such as congregational singing. Here is an instance where we lose ourself in ritual—it is not an individual thing—and yet we feel emotionally uplifted. By submitting to the form (the words, the tune) we are allowed an intensity of feeling that we should probably not feel otherwise. And our worship is multiplied because of it. Spontaneity—which in this case, I suppose, would mean everyone singing the hymn of his choice or humming a favorite top-forty tune—would ruin it. That would be the democratic thing to do, but it would be a foolish way to conduct a worship service.

Heaven is the place of true freedom, but it is not a democracy. Going your own way is not the chief virtue practiced there. And although the American spirit is not always a bad spirit to have, it is not the prevailing spirit in that place.

All of us who were brought up in America have been subject since birth to visions of wagon wheels moving west, the sound of train whistles calling, and songs of cowboys following their wandering stars. At the same time, we have this notion that a man isn't being sincere unless he's shouting or smiling. Very few of us have altogether escaped the effect of this. The idea of frontier spontaneity is still flitting about at the back of our minds and quite capable of masquerading as Christianity. It is part of our job as Christians to see that it does not.

CHAPTER 12

Secular Temptations

The argument to date says that Christians must be careful of confusing their faith both with psychological ideas and with cultural ones. Let's consider the consequences for Christianity when such confusion is allowed to stand. But first I should clear up a possible misunderstanding.

I have criticized the pioneer attitude in Christianity, and yet a few chapters before I had spoken of Christians as wanderers who must be ready to fling their packs on their backs. You are probably wanting to ask "What's the difference?" The difference is between the two views themselves. Either we are like frontiersmen and God is our laissez-faire president who has given us carte blanche to explore and open up the religious wilderness, or else we are like Bunyan's pilgrims on a journey with God as both our destination and our guide. The difference is that in the first case we may very well be traveling away from God. That attitude is not conducive to reverence. And while we may speak rather proudly of the irreverent American spirit, we should consider that an irreverent Christian spirit is a contradiction in terms.

The Secularization of Christians

The practical importance of neglecting the sacred, whether through too much psychology or too much of the American spirit, is to make Christianity more and more like the secular world around it. Does that sound odd? We are accustomed to hearing Christians condemn secularism in no uncertain terms; wouldn't it follow that they would be thoroughly armed against it? The answer is yes, if by secularism you only mean court rulings against religious practices or television's promoting dubious values. But secularism is more than that. Primarily it means judging by secular or worldly criteria rather than sacred ones. On that basis the Christian mind will often be found to be little different from the secular mind.

The problem can be illustrated on the one hand by evangelists who present Christianity as the key to worldly success or to physical health. There is nothing wrong with wanting to be successful or healthy, but these should be recognized as chiefly secular criteria. On the other hand it isn't a problem only for conservative-minded Christians. The liberal Christian whose mind is mainly on social justice or third world liberation is also measuring by worldly criteria—and they are very nearly the same criteria: namely material and social progress. Both left and right tend to promise a reward of earthly self-fulfillment for the right kind of Christian. And it should be noted that both usually tend toward a typically American impatience for results, and especially results of a sweeping and global nature.

Less serious than using worldly criteria, but still potentially harmful, is the practice of using worldly methods to achieve sacred ends. There is, for example, a disturbing similarity between the methods used by media evangelists and those used on ordinary talk shows or game shows. You have the toll-free numbers to call, the special tapes that will be rushed to you, the endorsements of athletes and businessmen, the Las Vegas style singers whose performance can be distinguished from secular ones only by the lyrics. It will be argued that such things are necessary. "We need to be relevant," they will say or, "We need to reach the young people." Most convincing of all is "These are the tactics that *work.*"

Perhaps it will seem I am putting the matter too strongly. It can be objected that there is really nothing very wrong with guitars or talk shows or Las Vegas singers. They have become an ordinary part of our daily life. But that is precisely the point. Because they are the stuff of ordinary life (or ordinary entertainment), we will want to use them sparingly, if at all. Too much of that approach and we quickly lose sight of the high and holy thing that the Christian faith is.

More of the Same or Something Different?

And there is this to consider. People turn to the Christian faith in the first place because they are looking for something more than the secular world has to offer; it is a disservice to give them back more of the same.

As for the argument about reaching the young people through relevance, well, that approach has already been tried and has been found to be a colossal failure. When liberal Catholic and Protestant educators tried their hand at being relevant, they succeeded only in hastening the departure of young people from their churches. It was relevant for the editors of one Catholic textbook to use three pages of advice from Carl Rogers's book *On Becoming Partners* as the basis for the chapter on marriage. It was equally relevant to present an episode from a popular television show in another such series. It is relevant also, I suppose, to put personality quizzes in Christian books or to run Sunday school discussion groups along encounter or values clarification models or to teach "decision-making skills." All of this is up-to-date and in tune, but what does it have to do with Christianity, which is timeless? Moreover, the tone is all wrong: it is much too familiar and worldly, too casual and irreverent. It is not a sacred tone.

Finally, it doesn't work. According to every index, these attempts at modernization only serve to weaken the faith of church members. Nor do they attract new members. When you end up telling the world what it already knows, it will have no further interest in listening to you.

Los Angeles and Loudun

The classic example of this misguided desire for relevance occurred in 1967 in Los Angeles when a large Catholic school system staffed by nuns invited Carl Rogers and his colleagues from the Western Behavioral Science Institute to carry on an experiment in "educational innovation" within their system. What ensued was an intense program of encounter groups lasting more than two years. It started off as one of those well-intentioned efforts we discussed in an earlier chapter, but the effect was not unlike the effect of inviting the devil into the convent at Loudun. At the beginning of the project there were six hundred nuns and fifty-nine schools: a college, eight high schools, and fifty elementary schools. A year following the project's completion, according to William Coulson, one of the project leaders, "there were two schools and no nuns."[1] The nuns had cut their ties with the Catholic church and had set themselves up as a secular order. From there, many drifted out of the religious life altogether.[2]

Although the events leading up to the secession were complicated by several factors, including the conservative nature of the Los Angeles archdiocese and a rising tide of feminism within some Catholic orders, there can be little doubt that Rogers's influence was a decisive, if not the decisive, element. Coulson, who seems to have mixed feelings about the outcome, gives the credit (or blame) to Rogers's group. "We did some job," he observed. Having read transcripts of parts of the encounter sessions, my own impression is that Rogers had effected something like a conversion. Many of the nuns confessed they had never felt so spiritually alive. Since I had been more or less converted to the faith of humanistic psychology merely by reading Rogers, I can well imagine the impact that two years of personal contact must have had.

Moses and Me-ism

I would not have been inclined to mention that incident were it not for the fact that the Catholic church is now taking steps to repair the damage done by secularization over the last twenty years. Nor would I have mentioned it if I did not think it was applicable to the church in general. Perhaps evangelical readers think the story has no bearing on them. If so, they should think again, for it is the very same sorts of theological and psychological experimentation to which many Catholics succumbed ten and fifteen years ago that now tempt the evangelical church.

The other day I picked from a rack in a Christian bookstore a booklet from a "Youth Bible Study" series for evangelical Christians. In the first chapter the following question appears: "Do you think Moses had a good image of himself or a bad image of himself?" Several more questions follow concerning Moses' self-image as well as the self-image of the reader.

The boy or girl who reads this will not lose faith because of it. But he or she will receive the impression that the point of Moses' life has mainly to do with learning self-esteem. (In a

Catholic text for students, the conversion of Saint Paul seems to take place for no other reason than to give him self-esteem and self-knowledge.)

Further on in this booklet, after the self-rating scales and the trust-walk exercise, the student is invited to give his opinion on a number of doctrinal questions. Included among them are: "I believe Jesus died and rose from the dead" versus "I can't believe Jesus came back to life after he was dead." The student indicates his belief by placing an "X" on a scale between the two views. Another choice is: "I believe Jesus is the Son of God" versus "I believe Jesus was a good man who lived a good life."

What can we make of this? The authors are without a doubt committed Christians. But at the same time they are trying very hard to be psychologically relevant. The result is a double message: the presentation of a Christian theme accompanied by a psychological theme or technique that only serves to undo it. The idea of presenting doctrines of the faith as a matter of choice clearly shows the influence of humanistic psychology. Since humanistic psychologists believe that truth is a personal construct, they are forced to utilize that kind of technique over and over. They have no other alternative but to encourage students to choose their own truths or values. But that is not the Christian position on truth. These techniques when used in Christian education will subtly condition youngsters to believe that faith is a matter of personal opinion.

The authors, unfortunately, are unaware of the incompatibility of the two approaches. They mainly have an eye to "reaching" the students. The actual message that reaches the student, however, is far different from what they think.

At a deeper level the cumulative effect of this booklet and others like it is to erase everything supernatural from the student's mind. I addressed this topic recently in another context, and what I said there seems to fit here: "The constant references to 'communications breakdowns,' 'risk taking,' 'involvement,' 'decision-making,' 'personhood,' 'I-you relationships,' 'getting in touch,' 'self-disclosure,' 'awareness,' and 'assertiveness' carries the implication that all the deep mysteries of faith can be encompassed in secular/psychological categories. In fact, there is very little sense that there are *any* deep mysteries—that there might be elements of the faith so awesome and unfathomable that they exist far beyond the reach of the social sciences."

It should be noted, however, that whatever success the social sciences have had in blurring the true nature of the faith has less to do with the force of their arguments than with their emotional appeal. Psychology's inroads into Christian life are due primarily to psychology's ability to offer emotional experiences sufficiently close to the experience of faith to be mistaken for faith itself. Because evangelical and charismatic Christians place such a great emphasis on the experience of faith, they are particularly susceptible to these imitations. That part of the world the Christian finds most attractive will often seem like Christianity itself. There will be much talk in it of brotherhood and love and the spirit. It will sound right. It will feel right. But it is wise to remind ourselves in the face of such temptation that the sacred can be drowned in a well of warm feelings just as surely as it can dry up in a secular desert.

Faith or Feelings?

When we reduce the importance of our faith to the feelings it produces in us, we are right back to the secular/psychological criterion. Surely that is not the standard that Christians want, for, among other things, it makes no allowance for the dark night of the soul—those dull, dry spells in faith that visit so many Christians (one is tempted to say, the best Christians) and last months or even years. Saints and mystics testify that this is a standard experience for them, and yet by the test of feeling good about ourselves it is an aberration. A thoughtful person, I think, will be forced to reject the test, because to accept this kind of criterion is to reject not only the experience of good Christians through the centuries but also to reject Christ's experience of His Father's absence as He hung on the cross. We are not to believe in God only so long as we can feel His presence. Indeed the real test of our faith is when we cannot feel it at all. The Scottish mystic George MacDonald, whom C. S. Lewis considered his spiritual father, wrote in this regard: "That man is perfect in faith who can come to God in the utter dearth of his feelings and desires, without a glow or an aspiration, with the weight of low thoughts, failures, neglects, and wandering forgetfulness, and say to Him, 'Thou art my refuge.'"

It makes sense to me that even the best Christian will have these experiences—just as even the best marriages have them. There are other things—duty, devotion, loyalty, and perseverance—that can carry us through in the absence of emotion. Love has to mature. It cannot be based on feelings alone, and often these dry spells are the thing that will move it onto higher and more solid ground. I sometimes think that God approaches us at first like a suitor. The initial effect on us can be akin to infatuation or young love. It is a roller coaster ride of emotion. But perhaps we are wrong to expect that the thrill must always be there, just as we would be wrong to expect a lasting marriage to be maintained on the romantic feelings of the couple when they first met.

CHAPTER 13

Answers to Suffering

The topic of this chapter is pain. If you are like me, you want to avoid it. But what do you do when it comes anyway? How do you explain the deaths in life that visit us despite our best efforts to sail away from them?

I am certainly not going to argue that we should go looking for pain. I take it for granted that we all want to subtract from the total of pain, not add to it. Neither am I going to argue that psychological approaches do not relieve pain. They sometimes do. The real test of a theory or way of life, however, is not whether it can relieve pain but what it says about the pain it cannot relieve. And this is where, I believe, psychology lets us down and Christianity supports us, for in psychology suffering has no meaning while in Christianity it has great meaning.

Now when you deprive someone of the sense that there is meaning in his suffering, you only compound the pain. Dumb, meaningless suffering is harder to take than suffering that seems to have a purpose. Injuries suffered as a result of carelessness are more galling than injuries suffered in a successful rescue attempt. Just remember how you felt the last time you carelessly smashed your thumb with a hammer, and compare that to how you would feel about a similar injury sustained while breaking down a door to free a child from a burning building. In the first case you will be inclined to curse your luck, and if you're like me, your mind will crowd with black and bitter thoughts about the absurd stupidity of life. In the second case you will be inclined to shrug off the pain. You will say, "It's nothing, really," and things of that sort because you can see your pain as a necessary part of a good deed.

By and large, psychology is forced into the first attitude about pain. No matter how gently it may proceed with your case, there will always be the implication that not only is your pain quite unfortunate but also quite useless; it doesn't do you or anyone else any good. In addition, you will be encouraged to believe that suffering is a mistake that can be avoided by rational living. "It's too bad you smashed your thumb," psychologists say in effect. "That was careless of you, or careless of your parents not to teach you proper hammering. But once you become fully aware and self-actualizing, you'll find that type of thing won't happen anymore. Let's see if we can't organize your life to avoid those mistakes."

What all this means, of course, is that your past suffering was worthless. The only good it has done, perhaps, has been to get you to the psychologist's office.

Is Suffering Wasted?

Christianity, on the other hand, says that suffering can be redemptive. Not all suffering, but any suffering that is joined to Christ's. That doesn't mean the church requires you to make a formal declaration of intent whenever you're in pain. The least hope or willingness that some good might be brought out of your misery is all God needs. The upshot is an attitude toward pain that is quite different from the psychological one. If you think your pain is senseless—in the same category with the carelessly mashed thumb—Christianity replies, "Don't be too sure. Don't be too sure you haven't been on some kind of rescue mission."

Now some Christians take a less radical view of this and say that the only purpose for our misfortunes is to get us into church or into reading the Bible—to bring us to our senses, in other words. But there is a problem with this view, because even after Christians have come to their senses they will still experience pain—and what is the good of that if the pain has already accomplished its purpose? Unless you are willing to say that God is wasteful of human suffering, I think you have to admit the possibility that a very high task accompanies our suffering. It is hard to imagine that God who suffered so much as a human has no other use for human suffering than as a corrective or prod to, so to speak, get us into His office.

There is a disagreement in theological circles about this matter, which I don't feel qualified to tackle, but it seems to me that all the best Christian thinkers have always suggested that while Christ's redemptive action on the cross was sufficient for all, God somehow allows us to participate through our own suffering in that redemptive act. It is a mystery of faith, of course, not a transparent thing. But something like that surely is the import of Christ's command to take up our cross and follow Him. As for Christ saying, "Greater love has no man than this, that a man lay down his life for his friends," what meaning can that have for us except on some supposition that we are to be joined in His work? There are not many opportunities for actually giving up our life for another; presumably our Lord meant also the daily sacrifices of our own good for the good of another. And presumably He did not mean we were to lay down our lives only that others might reap material success or good mental health.

Certainly His friends were no better off in material ways after His death. In fact, their sufferings had hardly begun until then.

So it seems that somehow our sufferings may, through Christ, work to the spiritual good not only of ourselves but of others. Charles Williams called this "the doctrine of substitution": that is, my life for yours, bearing one another's burdens, and even bearing those burdens without knowing it or knowing it only dimly. Christians believe they belong to a mystical body where each part of the body works to the good of every other part. But since it is a mystical body, we shouldn't expect to see all the ligaments and connecting tissues.

This is the Christian answer to suffering. Do you want to be of help in this universe? Well, perhaps you already are. Perhaps in some naive and heady youthful moment you asked God to use you for some good purpose. It may be that God has taken you at your word—although His way of using you is not at all what you bargained for. Perhaps right now there is someone you wish very much to help—possibly a friend or relative trapped in some ghastly situation or in his own miserable hate or pettiness. Perhaps you have tried to lend a hand and failed miserably. But what made you think it would be that easy? Possibly that is not the way the thing works. Perhaps the disappointments you endure and the heartaches you bear, although they seem unrelated to his case, are helping to do the job that your own efforts cannot. It all sounds beyond human reason, of course, but that is what you might expect from a God who becomes a man and offers up His life on a cross. "The Son of God suffered unto the death," wrote George MacDonald, "not that men might not suffer, but that their sufferings might be like His." It takes faith to believe something like that, but without such a belief, suffering makes no sense at all.

Born Too Soon?

Something else needs to be said here. Christianity is often contrasted unfavorably to humanism because humanists supposedly care more about people. You will hear it said that the humanist is more concerned with justice and the relief of suffering than the Christian who, it is argued, has given up on the world. This argument, of course, ignores the massive fact of practical Christian charity in the world—the schools, orphanages, hospitals, and relief services. But it does not even hold up on a theoretical level. It should be plain from the argument of the last several pages that the Christian attitude toward suffering is a good deal more humanistic than the humanist one. The humanist viewpoint is, in reality, the one that has given up on the world for it has absolutely nothing to say about the misery of the past. What good does it do to the billions who have already passed through this life in wretchedness, that scientific humanism will one day create a world without suffering? For that matter what good does it do to those who are right now dying miserable and lonely deaths all over the world? All that a strict humanism has to say to most of the human race living and dead is "Too bad you were born too early" and "Too bad about your suffering." The bulk of the world's pain is written off as a bad expense.

The Christian attitude, on the other hand, is not willing to come to terms with a scheme in which most of human travail means nothing and comes to nothing. Rather, Christians believe that God preserves every tear. Harry Blamires has said this much better than I can:

> If this life is the whole show, the man of conscience rejects it as one vast manifestation of injustice, one vast display of absurdity, if not of evil. If the experience between birth and death constitutes the sum total of the individual's conscious-

ness, then that total consciousness has in many cases been three parts unmerited misery, three parts undeserved pain. Does one want to be happy with a setup in which such is or has been the last word for a single human being? Does one want to enjoy food, music, or friendship in a setup which arbitrarily arranges that fellow creatures across the way, or across the world, shall have a total experience of consciousness which is largely privation, distress, or pain?[1]

A good man, he concludes, wants to see a good deal more justice than the humanist scheme provides.

Is Suffering Avoidable?

At several points in this book I have used the argument that the Christian explanation of things, with all its mystery, is much closer to a description of the way life is really experienced. I believe the same holds true with suffering. Christianity maintains that suffering is a necessary part of redemption. Because it is necessary for us, it follows that no matter how people organize their lives they will not be able to avoid it. And this seems to me a fairly accurate description of our experience. Our elaborate schemes for avoiding Scylla usually put us right in the path of Charybdis.

Psychology, as we have seen, has a different account of things. Suffering, it says, is a foolish mistake and, moreover, an avoidable one. Whether you go to a humanistic psychologist or a behaviorist or one who practices rational-emotive therapy, there will be this very strong suggestion that you can get control of your life and overcome your problems. Of course, to some extent you can. We are not completely helpless. The important question is, "To what extent?" Here, it seems to me, the answer of psychology is often quite unrealistic and quite unlike the stumbling, on-our-feet-and-off-again experience we have of life. If by "control" they mean "control our attitude," that would be one thing. But by "control" they often mean "control our fate." And that, I submit, is not a description of what life is like but a utopian description of what we would like it to be like.

There is one significant exception to this among psychologists—the existential psychologists. The Austrian psychiatrist Victor Frankl is the best example here. He emphasizes that any of us may be faced with a fate we can no longer change, in which case the important thing is the stand we take toward it. His excellent book, *Man's Search For Meaning,* is really a book about finding meaning in suffering. But it is important to realize that Frankl did not derive his ideas from psychology so much as he did from his experiences in a Nazi concentration camp and from his exposure to Judaism and Christianity.

Then, too, he is European. In America the idea of a fate you cannot change does not wash well. What we have instead is an idea as American as Coca Cola—positive thinking. It is the standard formula for most of the paperback self-help and psychology books that reach popular audiences. With enough positive thinking, according to this view, you can control events. It is all up to you whether misfortune comes your way or not. In short, everything is in your head.

Quite obviously, such an attitude can become widespread only in a subjectivist climate. It denies any real importance to the objective events that take place outside our mind. And yet, surprisingly, it is widely accepted. Just the other week I was arguing the point with a young man who insisted that we have almost total control over the events of our lives. The irony is that he had just lost his job, smashed his car beyond repair because the brakes failed, and a week subsequent to our conversation was asked to leave the rooming house where he was staying.

[187]

The other side of positive thinking is the belief that negative things happen because we have a negative outlook. Well, once again, that is sometimes true; but just as often our negative outlook is the result of prior misfortunes, not the cause of them. It is not always just in your head. Bad things do happen, in very concrete and intractable ways.

The Case of the Missing Body

We have all seen mystery movies where someone, usually a young woman, has witnessed a murder or discovered a body. But while she rushes off to find help, the body is removed. When she returns with the police, they refuse to believe her. "But it was right here," she insists. "I saw it!" The police are still disbelieving, but they are polite. "Look," says one of the detectives, "sometimes our minds can play tricks on us. I don't believe you're lying. I believe that you believe you saw a body."

We, the audience, are of course pulling for the woman who, as the only witness to the crime, is herself now in danger; and we are aghast at the stupidity and condescension of the police who seem more concerned with protecting her feelings than exploring the facts of the case. We know that she is right, and they are wrong. We know that somewhere there is a real body and that *it* is the cause of her disturbance.

Now change the situation somewhat, and put the young lady in a psychologist's office. Let us say she suffers from feelings of loneliness. She thinks the problem is simple bad luck. She's never found the right man. It's the case of the missing body again. Or is it as simple as that? The psychologist is polite but disbelieving: "Your problem is not that you can't find somebody. The problem is in your attitude. You don't believe enough in yourself."

At this point the woman may protest feebly that she had always believed in herself, but after a while the loneliness began to tell. But the counselor prevails: "I believe you believe you need a boyfriend, but what you really need is self-confidence. Once you get that, you won't have any trouble attracting others."

Do you see how—once we've made a psychological problem out of it—this changes our response? However much our sympathy may lie with the movie heroine who insists that there actually is a missing body, we tend to be suspicious of the client who can't find a body to love. We don't root for her the way we do for the damsel in distress. We do tend to think it's her own fault. She has the wrong attitude toward life. She hasn't practiced positive thinking.

Adding Insult to Injury

Taking a positive mental attitude sometimes creates changes, and sometimes it does not. When it does not, and if we have let ourselves believe that lack of competence is at the root of our problem, two consequences will follow. In the first place our suffering is trivialized. Although some of our problems come from stupidity or selfishness on our part, many come because we have tried to do something worthwhile such as create a family and provide for it. Most of us struggle and sacrifice for people or causes outside ourselves, and sometimes even at the cost of our self-interest. We may risk suffering for the sake of a child, for the sake of a parent, even for God's sake. From time to time we overextend ourselves and end up face down in the dust, confused and discouraged, our best efforts defeated. Not all our problems, in short, are clinical problems, but sometimes simply the surest sign that we are human.

From the psychological view, however, we are forced to

reinterpret our plight as a sickness rather than a spiritual struggle. Real human problems are trivialized by reducing them to pathologies, thus robbing our everyday struggles of any dignity or meaning. And a suggestion that our problems can be solved by this or that simple method may only serve to further belittle them.

Paul Vitz puts this rather well:

> What does one say to the older worker who has lost his job, whose skills are not wanted? What does one tell the woman who is desperately alone inside an aging body and with a history of failed relationships? Does one advise such people to become more autonomous and independent? Does one say "go actualize yourself in creative activity"? For people in those circumstances such advice is not just irrelevant, it is an insult."[2]

The other consequence is to compound our sense of worthlessness. Suppose after five years of therapy you still can't manage your life. You have tried this and that technique; you have read self-help books. And perhaps for a while things did improve. And then, just when you saw your life coming together again, something unexpected happened and the whole thing fell apart. Well, whose fault is that?

Be sure that your therapist won't take the blame. He knows there's nothing wrong with his theories or his techniques. Indeed, he is probably becoming annoyed with you. Few will actually say this, but it is quite true that counselors do lose patience with clients who seem to make no progress or make the same mistakes over and over. And from their point of view it is an understandable irritation since, by and large, they do not believe in original sin and, by and large, their theories won't let them believe the human situation is quite as desperate as Christianity says it is.

So there it is. We supposedly have great potential for overcoming. But the result of this is not a lessening of guilt. Since no one ever stops to question the basically trouble-free scenario that psychology proposes to be within our grasp, we can only conclude that it is we who are at fault, and we will only grow more bitter over the seemingly absurd anguish of our lives.

By contrast, the Christian view provides no utopian scheme of what our lives could be like, but a concrete explanation of why they are the way they are. That is why G. K. Chesterton could say that the doctrine of original sin was the most cheerful idea he knew of. If one takes the Christian view and accepts sin, failure, and shortcoming as the common lot of a fallen race rather than a personal inadequacy, the burden of guilt becomes more bearable and understandable.

But we can't merely leave it at that.

Misguided Christian Notions

We started several chapters ago with the intention of disentangling Christian notions from psychological ones. This means that if we are going to criticize certain psychological ideas we must equally criticize them when they show up wearing Christian garb. If we are honest we have to admit that many Christians also have a great faith in positive thinking. It was a Christian minister, after all, who coined the term "the power of positive thinking." You may want to object that with Christians it is not the same thing. But in point of fact it often is: it is faith in self rather than faith in God.

Norman Vincent Peale's philosophy, for example, comes perilously close to a faith in the sheer power of believing. The object of faith seems almost secondary. Although Peale wants us to believe in God, he seems primarily concerned with belief as a psychological mechanism for achieving successful living. And he puts an extraordinary emphasis on believing in ourselves. You find the same attitude in some of the media evangelists. Some talk about the power of belief, some talk about "possibility thinking," and they nearly always talk about prosperity. The point here is that this attitude is remarkably similar to the attitude of popular psychology: belief is pragmatic; certain beliefs are useful in producing positive mental states; and positive mental states produce prosperity. Believe and grow rich, or believe and overcome your troubles—that sort of thing.

Even when the positive-thinking Christian places his faith in God, it is sometimes a very presumptive faith. You may be told by some Christians that you have "a claim on Christ," and the sense of it is often that God is obligated to answer our prayers exactly to our satisfaction, as though we were filing a claim with an insurance company. Now this may be biblical in the sense that you can find one or two passages to lend support to it, but it is not biblical if you look at the whole and obvious testament of the Scriptures. The characters in the Bible are not as a rule people who received success in life— certainly not worldly success. "Listening to the disciples," writes David Myers, "one hears no glamorous testimonies of 'how I overcame anger, selfishness, and doubt.'"[3] What you get, rather, is a record of constant temptation, backsliding, and struggle.

I am not saying God does not perform miracles, nor do I deny that in some cases He may shower us with worldly blessings. He may grant us such things from time to time "in order that you may believe," or for some other reason best known to Him. But that is up to God. And He is the God of Abraham, Isaac, and Jacob, not a slot machine.

The problem that crops up here is the same problem that afflicts the victim of popular psychology. Suppose after putting your faith in the Lord you still have that arthritis or cancer? What then? Does it mean you haven't prayed hard enough? Does it mean something is wrong with your faith? And isn't it, finally, a form of Pelagianism—a way of thinking that God can be bought if you can ante up sufficient personal effort? That attitude, you must remember, was the one the Reformers attacked most strongly. The proper Christian emphasis is not on *our* efforts, *our* abilities, or even *our* faith. It is on our faith in *God*.

Giving Tragedy Its Due

A final note. Even when we do get rid of one problem, another usually takes its place. After this, there remains the fact that some problems are insoluble. They don't go away. Psychology doesn't like to admit that fact, because it can offer no consolation in the face of it. Hence, in the manuals of popular psychology we find a heavy emphasis on being a winner, because only a winner can celebrate. If you are a loser—if you can't beat your problems—you are totally, utterly lost. Consequently, you must strive to be a winner at any cost. The notion that the losers of this world might have anything to celebrate is incomprehensible to the psychological mind. And yet, there is another tradition that allows even the losers to be festive. From another point of view—a truly Christian one—there is cause to rejoice even if you can't handle your problems.

This, I think, is because Christianity gives tragedy its due. It seems paradoxical, but when we trivialize suffering and tragedy we also trivialize the experience of happiness. Where suffering is looked upon as some kind of mistake, those who suffer can never be very happy about their lives. Where a Christian view prevails, however, even the poorest of the poor may occasionally rejoice.

The gaiety surrounding Christmas and other feast days attests to this. The poorest quarter of the poorest town in the poorest country will come alive at these times. Perhaps this was more true in the past—before the poor along with everyone else learned that the point of life is to be fulfilled in a material sense. And perhaps these vigorous celebrations were and are sometimes occasions for rowdy horseplay as well as holiness, for drunkenness as well as devotion. But it does seem that what makes them possible at all is a religious faith at the heart of which is the recognition of a darkness far darker and a glory far brighter than anything the psychological society has yet revealed to us.

Something to Celebrate

Auguste Comté, who is generally credited as the founder of the religion of humanism, wanted to establish new humanist feast days to replace the Christian ones, which he was sure would die out. G. K. Chesterton, the great English apologist, professed disappointment that none were forthcoming. He would be glad, he said, for an excuse for another celebration, and "could easily imagine myself with the greatest enthusiasm lighting a bonfire on Darwin Day." But, of course, Comté and his followers failed in their effort: "They have not," chided Chesterton, "set up a single new trophy or ensign for the world's merriment to rally to. They have not given a name or a new occasion of gaiety." One does not, as he observed, "hang up his stocking on the eve of the birthday of Victor Hugo" or ". . . sing carols descriptive of the infancy of Ibsen outside people's doors in the snow."[4]

Were Chesterton alive today I think he might profess the

same mock disappointment with the religion of psychology. Whatever its other virtues, and despite its claim to psychic liberation, psychology fails somehow to bring out our festive nature. We do not—if I might extend Chesterton's analogy—exchange presents or greeting cards on the birth-day of Dr. Freud or dance in a circle on the anniversary of his discovery of the unconscious. We do not have solemn pro-cessions or sing hymns on Jung Day, though Jung would certainly have approved. The memory of Pavlov does not put a spring in our step, nor do we let loose streamers or set off firecrackers in commemoration of Stimulus-Response Day. We do not eat roast turkey or pass the punch bowl on the Feast Day of Abraham Maslow, nor do we decorate eggs and hunt for them on Human Potential Day.

Despite our faith in the theology of psychology, we do not find much cause for rejoicing in it. We do not do so today, and it seems safe to say that two thousand years hence we still will not.

CHAPTER 14

Like Little Children

We have developed a habit in our society of judging an idea not on its merits but on the sentiments it arouses in us. We will elect a president not because we have thoroughly grasped the issues at stake in an election but because this man strikes us as compassionate or that man strikes us as honest. One of the main reasons for the popularity of psychology lies here. It manages to arouse the proper sentiments in us: it seems to be on the side of the angels.

More Counterfeit Christianity

This is particularly true of psychology's ideas about children. Those ideas appear to strike the right note—the right note for Christians anyway. In much psychological writing and thinking there is an echo of Christ's admonition to become like little children—not in so many words, of course, but in the suggestion that there is something special and wondrous about children and in the further suggestion that adults have something of great value to learn from them. So there are two points of similarity: children possess certain virtues in an exceptional degree; and ideas about children are, when properly understood, ideas about what adults should be like. These apparent similarities only add to the confusion Christians have about psychology.

I want to argue, however, that there is actually very little similarity in ideas here, only a similarity of sentiment. The shopper next to you in the bookstore may be stocking up on *The Magic Years, Peter Pan,* and stuffed unicorns, but there is still no reason to suppose that his ideas about children coincide with yours. His heart may be in the right place, but you can't conclude that his head is. And if the head isn't in the right place, it is often a good bet that the heart won't be there for long either. This is one reason why Christianity insists on doctrine: it's a corrective to wandering sentiment.

When psychology errs, it is usually a matter of having its head in the wrong place, not its heart. Nevertheless, it won't do to be ruled by sentiment in such an important matter as understanding children and rearing them. The fact that you have a special reverence for children doesn't mean you will do them any good. If your ideas aren't sound, you may even do them harm. It's important to be clear, then, about what psychologists mean when they hold up children for our imitation. It is usually not at all what Christians mean.

The real question at work here is what accounts for the happiness of children. Of course, you first have to grant that children *are* happier than adults. That seems more doubtful now than it did just a short time ago, and there are always disturbing exceptions to the rule, but I think we can still call it the rule. Just ask yourself whether you would rather have the task of getting a child out of a depressed mood or an adult. The child can easily be distracted with a story or an ice cream. If these things fail, you can always tickle him. With an adult it is not so easy; the mood is generally deeper and darker. At any rate, if we concede the point about the child's greater happiness, our next step is to examine the differences between the psychological explanation and the Christian one. There are four distinctions to be made.

Four Differences

1. A good deal of psychological thinking about children comes under the heading of naturalism—the conviction that the spontaneous, unsolicited way is always the right way. In this view nature knows best, and innocent children who are supposed to live closer to the state of nature are gifted with that natural wisdom. The way to a healthier, more uninhibited life, then, is to become more childlike. Along with this view goes a lot of talk about how children are like seedlings or buds who will naturally bloom into flowers if adults don't thwart their growth. The implication is that adults, too, have a child within that has probably not been allowed to unfold, and with which the wise adult will want to get back in touch.

The Christian position, by contrast, says that these little flowers of the field need cultivation. It isn't enough just to let them grow. A good gardener will not stand by and watch weeds and insects take over the garden, and a good parent will not let a child tend his own nursery. The difference between the two viewpoints is considerable. The first places a faith in human nature that most people are unwilling to put in nature herself; the second assumes that children like everyone else are fallen: some of their instincts are healthy and need to be cultivated, others are not and need to be discouraged. If there is a lesson to learn from children, naturalism is not it.

2. Another supposition in psychological thinking is that the child is happier because he is freer. Freer, that is, to express himself—not to pretend to like squash, as an adult dinner guest might feel constrained to do; freer from convention—to be able to turn his interest to his toy truck once adult conversation grows boring; freer from worry and responsibility—no bills to pay, no dinners to prepare. And the message for adults? Quite obviously, free yourself.

Except—and here is where the Christian view comes in—when adults act on this message and free themselves, it is children who will always pay the price. A moment's reflection tells us this is so. It makes a tremendous difference to a boy's or girl's happiness when his or her parents begin to flirt with freedom. It is at that precise point where the father or mother declares his or her freedom from the family that the freedoms of the child are reduced to nearly nothing. I mean freedom from insecurity, from doubt, from fear. The truth is that a child's happiness is much less likely to be linked to his freedom, which after all is quite limited, than to his sense that he belongs to a secure and ordered system. He is free to play at knights or cowboys because the gates of his castle or fort are kept by sturdy guardians. He is free to let his fantasies roam because he has a pair of mighty jinn to conjure up meals three times a day. No matter how much he may complain about the privileges of his older brother, or wonder aloud why he can't stay up like his parents, nine-tenths of his felicity comes from having a snug place in a roofed and four-walled hierarchy. And this brings us along to another curious omission in the psychologist's account of things.

3. There can exist side by side in a certain kind of person a desire for childhood innocence along with a complete disdain for authority. Any number of self-help writers will encourage you to become more childlike and trusting, and yet at the same time insist that you brook no interference in your life from any source. You are to be wide-eyed and guileless, and at the same time as independent as any sea captain. Nearly every reader will have read this kind of advice or met the kind of person who believes it. And very patiently we must remind them that they have conveniently forgotten a large fact: little children do not get on very well in the world without mothers and fathers. To suppose that you can have the special freedom of the adult and the special happiness of

the child is a confusion of two different worlds. The point is this: much of the sentimental talk about returning to childhood that we hear from popular psychologists and others is based on incompatible expectations. It may sound Christian, but it is nothing like Christianity—nothing like common sense for that matter. They want to be like little children, but they don't want a father. They may as well go to a restaurant and order soup without the bowl.

All of which is to say that they have latched on to some fetching ideas but have not bothered to think them through. Christianity, on the other hand, holds you to certain realistic requirements. There is in the long run, it says, only one way to regain the trustfulness and bliss of children and that is to have a Father in heaven. The most consistent image of God in the New Testament is the image of Him as a Father; the most consistent image of us is as His children. This can only mean that God wants of us the same obedience that we ask of our children, but it also means that just as our children are dependent on us for all their needs, we can depend on God our Father for all of ours. And just as we want our children to trust us, we should trust God. This is not easy. Like the child who does not understand why his father has to put a stinging antiseptic on his bruised knee, we may not understand everything our heavenly Father does for our good. Like any good father He will go ahead and give us the first aid we need despite our whining and protests, but how much better for us to display that trust in Him that we are so pleased to see in our own children.

Some people will find it hard to understand how dependence and obedience go together with joy. They have probably been misled by too many stories of the "bad boy" type so common in American fiction—that is, the bad boy who seems to have so much fun. They should take a closer look at real life bad boys. More often than not they will find, an inch below that ruddy, grinning surface, a driven compulsion to escalate every matter out of all proportion until it finds arms and hearts strong enough to contain it. The child who has the true spirit of obedience has, by contrast, a lightheartedness that his reckless companion can seldom attain. The one has the fun of disobeying, the other has what literary critic Roger Sale calls "the deeper delight of obeying."

4. There is nothing more telling in the difference between the Christian and psychological views about returning to childhood than the respective paths we are advised to follow. With psychology it is the path of bigness; with Christianity, the path of smallness. Much psychological advice centers around ways to increase your self-esteem, enhance your self-worth, and so on. "You are the most important person in the world"—that sort of thing. Christ, on the other hand, told us to become like *little* children.

Now the average man can understand the advantage of having back the child's easy laughter and quick delight—but littleness? What's the advantage in that? Chesterton once gave a good answer to this question by weaving a story about two boys, Peter and Paul. Both were offered a wish in the standard manner of the fairy tale, and Paul wished to become a giant "that he might stride across continents." And so he did. Only when he came to the Himalayas they seemed no more interesting than the miniature rockery in the family garden; and Niagara "was no bigger than the tap turned on in the bathroom." Peter, obviously the wiser of the two boys, made the opposite request. He asked to be small— "about half an inch high." Since the boys had been standing in the front garden, he now found himself "in the midst of an immense plain, covered with a tall green jungle above which, at intervals, rose strange trees each with a head like the sun. . . . Toward the middle of this prairie stood up a mountain of such romantic and impossible shape, yet of such stony height and dominance that it looked like some incident of the end of the world." Peter "set out on his adventures across that coloured plain; and he has not come to the end of it yet."[1]

Reading this reminds us that the literature of smallness is always a literature of adventure: Gulliver among the giants, *The Incredible Voyage,* and those delightful scenes in *The Once and Future King* where Arthur is allowed to see life from the perspective of a fish or insect. Looked at from the right angle "the grass is an everlasting forest with dragons for denizens" (Chesterton again). The right angle of course is humility. It puts you in a position to see how wondrous things are.

Splendor in the Grass

The really wholesome element in the psychologist's view of children is that many of them do see this wonder and give it its due. The problem is, they are hard put to account for it. The best they can come up with is an explanation that hinges on the newness and freshness of the child's perceptions. Let us see if we can do better than that. And let us start where we left off a few sentences ago—in the grass.

There is a famous line in one of Wordsworth's poems in which he speaks of "splendor in the grass." He meant the splendor he recollected from childhood. If we make a mental effort, I think we can understand what it was he referred to. Did you ever as a child lie in tall grass and simply watch? Down on that level, if the grass is high enough, it does take on the appearance of Chesterton's "everlasting forest." You may peer between the blades as if through a forest glade and observe goings-on that are hidden from adult eyes. The small forest creatures are there, and the large green dragons that prey upon them.

Was it not a wonder that such things existed at all? Well, perhaps for you it was not the grass. Perhaps you were the indoor type and found your splendor (let us say) lying on the oriental rug, where you could nestle down on the level of tuft and fibre, and where, in your imagination, you might even venture into the paths of that exotic and patterned forest. Or perhaps your reverie had as its starting point a set of ceramic figurines, or a glass paperweight embedded with flowers, or an old mahogany desk with brass pulls, cubbyholes, and keyholed drawers. Any one of these things might open another world.

But that is not all. About all these common things (and remember, you are very young) there clung . . . well, it is difficult to say exactly *what* it was. Wordsworth spoke of meadows and groves "apparelled in celestial lights." Others have spoken of an aura surrounding objects. Let it suffice to say that for the very young child even material objects may seem to be alive or have a spirit about them. If I try hard enough I can remember from my earliest childhood a certain house (or it may have been only a picture of a house), one side of which was built up out of the water with moss covering the brownstone at the water line. For me that house was a mythic thing that seemed to live and breathe; not only the moss but the whole house appeared drenched with what I can only call liquid significance. There is something else to add: the place seemed to speak of a vast antiquity—a concept I should have had no familiarity with at that age. And, what's more, it seemed I had seen it before—long ago.

Memories of Paradise?

Now one of the curious things about the type of experience we are discussing is that, no matter how strange, it is often accompanied by a feeling of recognition, of déjà vu, of having been there before. For example, a close reading of Wordsworth's poetry suggests that what he remembers is itself a remembering—a memory of a memory. It was not simply his childhood contact with nature he recalls but something farther off, beyond or behind nature. You see this also in Lewis's account of a recollected boyhood experience that stirred a memory of bliss "from a depth not of years but of centuries."

The most famous explanation of this phenomenon is Plato's doctrine of recollection. It is not, from a Christian view, a completely satisfying account, but it is a good starting point. Plato believed that prior to birth individuals preexist in a heavenly state—what he called the world of Eternal Forms. There they are in direct contact with the true essence of things: not this or that particular truth but the very source of truth, not this or that particular beauty but Beauty itself. The world we are born into is only a dim reflection of the heavenly world; still, it is a reflection, and this accounts for the strange familiarity of things we see for the first time. But the older we grow, the dimmer it becomes. For the child who has only recently arrived from the place of Eternal Forms, earthly things will stir a more vivid memory. He will have a more urgent pang of recollection, a more poignant stab of joy. But as he grows older and travels farther away from his origins, things lose their splendor and power of evocation. Their celestial halo fades "into the light of common day."

Occasionally adults experience a return of this splendor. The sun strikes the water in a particular way or an old melody reaches your ear, and you feel yourself in the presence of something immensely big, some sort of tremendous enlightenment seems to be rushing at you. Or you taste a home-baked cruller, and suddenly you are back in your grandmother's kitchen and the world seems very large and full of possibilities again. But whatever is there is gone as soon as it is found. Years may pass before it happens again.

It is that sort of thing that makes us yearn for the magic days of childhood. And even if we no longer feel it in ourselves, we can still see the wonder in a child's eyes or hear it in his voice. It is not necessary to adopt Plato's explanation of this yearning. His value is in recognizing the yearning and attempting to offer an explanation. A Christian view would simply say that the child sees things for what they are. Not that we pre-existed but that the wonder is always there. For those who have eyes to see, the grass and trees will always carry a hint of their Creator's presence; the woods will always be sacred woods. The sense of déjà vu may be not a memory of some past Eden but a premonition of Paradise, an intuition of the place we truly belong to. "Ever since the creation of the world," wrote Saint Paul, "his invisible nature, namely, his eternal power and deity, has been clearly perceived in the things that have been made."

But why don't we clearly perceive? Our own experience of these blissful moments gives us a clue why they are so rare for us and so common for children. They are moments of self-forgetfulness. They are accompanied by a loss of interest in the self and a complete absorption in something better. An emptying out occurs that is not our own accomplishment. I would use the word *possession* if it did not have the wrong connotations. It would have to be understood in this instance as a divine possession. The experience signifies that something or someone else has taken hold. For this reason attempts at self-mastery or self-control are out of place here. To get into this realm one has to leave that sort of thing at the door.

Two Lessons

Two lessons can be drawn from this. The first regards the psychological idea of recapturing the child within. Psychologists who promote this idea really ought to be more careful about the terms they employ. Become like a child? Splendid. From a Christian point of view, imperative. But to really do it means abandoning the greater part of the psychological program, especially that part that focuses on self-enlargement. If you insist you are God's gift to the world, you are in a poor position to recognize and receive God's gifts to you.

The second lesson regards the use of drugs. It seems plain to me that much drug use, whether consciously or not, is an attempt to regain something lost with childhood. Drug users will talk glowingly of the vividness of colors, of material objects seeming to come alive, of experiencing a stretched-out sense of time not unlike the child's (remember how a summer seemed an eternity?). And, of course, it is true that you can knock the ego out of commission by artificial means and thereby open yourself up to uncommon experiences. But surely it ought to tell us something about our condition if we go about it this way. The adolescent or adult needs expensive chemicals and assorted paraphernalia; the child does it with lightning bugs, morning frost, or the dog next door. There is nothing humble about the first way; it's a presumptive attempt to grab at experience and make it come at your bidding.

The approach is wrong, moreover, because these experiences are not meant to be ends in themselves but only clues or pointers to something beyond. They are the fringes of glory, not glory itself, and if you do not go beyond the experiences to the reality toward which they point, the fringes will become worn and faded. You will try more and more desperately to recapture something that cannot be recaptured but is yet to be discovered. By their very nature these experiences say to us "I am not the thing you want, only its messenger." Having said that, it has served its purpose: a purpose we defeat by focusing on the messenger and ignoring the message. Lewis, who seemed to have the sort of experience through reading poetry and myth that others have from drugs, came to this conclusion after his conversion. "It was valuable," he wrote, "only as a pointer to something other and outer. While that other was in doubt, the pointer naturally loomed large in my thoughts. When we are lost in the woods the sight of a signpost is a great matter." But one does not waste his time staring at signposts when the road is plain and when, as Lewis says, "We would be at Jerusalem."[2]

A Canopy of Order

The joy of childhood is not something you go after directly by trying to recreate childhood experiences like some grownup sneaking into the nursery to steal a ride on the rocking horse. The preservation of it seems to turn rather on what might at first seem its opposite: duty, restraint, and beyond that the conscious maintenance of the distinction between child and adult. Adults have the light of revelation and no longer need the celestial light. The more they pay attention to the claims of Christian duty, the more they will forget themselves and find, by a paradox, that in becoming more adult they have become more childlike, and therefore capable of the child's joy. The child, in turn, needs adults strong enough to erect over his head a canopy of order and serenity. His right is to be filled with wonder, not worry. After that, the task of leading him from natural revelation to divine revelation will be an easier one.

We should indeed become like little children, but we should be clear what we mean by this. The happiness of children (and their particular virtue) comes not from their freedom, or from their self-awareness, or from their self-esteem (these are all adult and adolescent preoccupations) but from their sense of marvel and from the security that a properly ordered adult society provides.

CHAPTER 15

Love

In earlier chapters I maintained that the Christian explanation of things fits our experience more closely than other accounts. I believe the same holds true of the Christian explanation of love. Contrary to a popular notion, the church is neither overly sentimental about weddings, nor overly narrow about sex, but simply very realistic about both.

Two Sides of Love

Our experience of love is two-sided. Most of us have had a taste of romance and found in it something far surpassing ordinary life. We told ourselves, "This is the way life ought to be!" and we were determined that was the way we would live it. In due time most of us found that romance did not live up to its promises. Some of us dropped the matter right there and became cool and calculating about the pursuit of the opposite sex. Others struggled on past romantic disappointments and fade outs to a more mature love. But even that, it turned out, was a much more difficult thing than one would have expected even in one's wisest moments.

That, if I am not wide of the mark, is the ordinary experience of love. To do it justice you need an explanation that doesn't deny meaning to either set of facts. That explanation can be found in what Christians refer to as the marriage of Christ and His church. Married love and all the steps leading up to it are a symbol of Christ's love for his bride, the church. More than that, it is a participation in that sacred marriage. That is why Saint Paul called it "a high mystery." In the Christian view of things the Gospels tell a love story about a bridegroom (Christ) who chooses for himself a rather unlikely prospect of a bride (us) and proceeds to make her over so that she will become "without spot or wrinkle." Part of the Book of Revelation is devoted to describing what the wedding feast will be like.

To a non-Christian or a lukewarm one, this surely sounds mysterious, if not far-fetched. Christian teachers have always replied, "Yes, it sounds mysterious, but unless love and marriage are treated as mysteries they simply do not work." This doesn't mean, by the way, that non-Christian marriages don't work. The important thing is to have a respect for the sacredness and mystery of the marriage bond. Most peoples down through history *have* treated it that way.

But I am drifting from the point. Only a doctrine like the marriage of Christ and the church will let you take seriously both your youthful romantic flights and the checkered patches of light and shade that make up a marriage. Ronald Knox, in an amusing yet instructive passage, has the church saying to the engaged couple, "Oh, you want to get married, do you? That means, you want to imitate the action of Jesus Christ in His Incarnation. Well, God bless you; you will want all the grace I can rout out for you if you are to do that, a whole trousseau of graces."[1]

Naturally, few of us have anything like that in mind. But what we generally find in marriage is that, if it's going to work, it will exact from us a good deal of sacrifice. In innumerable and unspectacular (sometimes spectacular) ways, couples find themselves laying down their lives for one another: giving up this plan; foregoing that event; taking out time they had meant to devote to this pleasant routine.

When you vow yourself to another, your self is really no longer your own; you will either have to die to it or see your marriage come apart. Jesus commanded His disciples to "love one another as I have loved you." They didn't know it at the time, but it turned out that "as I have loved you" meant "unto death." Dare we say that in marriage—particularly in marriage—we are given the privilege of loving as Christ loved?

A Greater Romance

Such weighty matters may seem miles away from romantic love with its rash vows and fervid testaments, and yet in a sense it is a piece of the same fabric. The church doesn't belittle your romantic impulse by calling it adolescent or foolish. She looks at your reckless, don't-count-the-cost brashness and says: "Good. You have the right attitude toward love. That is exactly the kind of abandon and dedication you will need. You are ready to meet any obstacle, make any sacrifice? Good. That is the way Christ loves His people."

The church says a number of other things as well. When hearts are broken or promises fade or the whole show simply does not live up to its billing, she will remind you that none of your earthly loves could possibly fill your yearning. You are meant for a greater romance. In short, romantic love, like other things, is seen properly when it is seen as a pointer or guide. It is meant to teach us that what we are looking for is to be found elsewhere. Not that the church doesn't take our vows and protestations seriously. If we are not careful we will find that she has taken us at our word. The church, wrote Chesterton, respects a man to the extent that it will "write his oath upon the heavens" and then ask him to live up to it. The church doesn't force the oath on us—lovers who carve their initials in oak or set them in cement don't do so under the prompting of the local pastor—it merely validates our natural inclination and sets a sacred seal on it.

Beyond Natural Love

Sooner or later when we find what Lewis in *The Four Loves* called "the unmistakable evidence that [natural] love is not going to be 'enough,' " the church reminds us that in getting married we have set a supernatural course. Our loves need to be born again along with our lives. Our natural love has to be transformed into a Christian virtue because love needs more than love itself to remain loving.

Few persons newly in love can be persuaded of that, of course. Like anything else, one can be prideful of one's ability to love. The young person's attitude is often something like, "I don't need any help; my love is strong enough by itself." So while they are perfectly willing to make their own pledges of faithfulness, they may not see any necessity for doing it before God and in a church. Their position is rather like the one most of us have toward ourselves as long as things are going our way. We can take care of ourselves, we think; we're O.K. as we are, without this business of being born again.

With that, we are back to the psychological view. But before plunging in, let us review the major point of the last several pages. Christianity does not deny the truth of our experience of love. In romance we feel that we have found or nearly found the highest thing; in mature love we find we have to do some of the hardest things. Christianity attributes this dual aspect to the fact that we are being prepared as a bride for her bridegroom. That means we must be formed to the point where we can begin to love as Christ loves. And

Christ loved us with a passion—that is, both with intense desire and intense suffering.

When the psychological world talks of love, however, it means nothing of this sort. Although they may have a good deal to say about love (and much that is sound as far as it goes), you will not find many psychologists staking your happiness on love the way Christianity does. Faced with the same set of facts as Christians, the psychological world usually decides that the stakes are too high. The psychologist can see as plainly as anyone that romantic love is usually a disaster and that married love can be a larger catastrophe. Having no more than natural tools at his disposal, he is not going to ask you to stake your all on love or cast your fate to the wind (as Christians are supposed to cast theirs on the Holy Spirit). But in taking this quite prudent stand, he is simultaneously forced to ask you to set aside the truth of your experience.

What Romantic Love Teaches Us

For example, one of the truths we experience in romantic love—and especially when our hearts are broken—is that we are incomplete in ourselves. We are, as Lewis put it, "one vast need." Our intuitive feeling when we are in love is that we were only half-living up to the moment we fell in love. We realize then how much our wholeness depends on someone outside ourselves. Take away our love, and we feel reduced to almost nothing. What a large emptiness resides in us when we are all by ourselves.

Now Christianity says that in this altered state we are getting a peek at the real nature of things—our emptiness without God, our complete dependence on Him for fulfillment. Psychology, on the other hand, has little choice except to tell you you were wrong to think yourself incomplete; people can and should be *self*-fulfilled. You were mistaken to depend on someone else. It's unhealthy to be that way. If you "reach deep down inside," you will find the wholeness you need.

But becoming self-sufficient doesn't mean you won't have love. Psychology is reassuring on that point. You will be more capable of giving love and receiving it. All this will follow naturally from your self-improvement like the clear weather that follows a rise in air pressure. Once you don't need love, you will have it.

B-Love and D-Love

This attitude explains why there is a great disdain in some psychological circles (and it has spread to feminist circles) for need love. Ever since Abraham Maslow made a distinction between "B-love' (love that flows from the fullness of your being and needs nothing in return) and "D-love" (a need for love based on a deficiency in you), psychologists have lined up on the side of B-love. For example, Fritz Perls felt that lovers should have no expectations of each other. Erich Fromm believed that mature love was marked by a disinterested appreciation. Like God on the sixth day, you simply note that other people exist and say that it is good. To put it another way, love means to affirm others in their being; the chief way to do this is to let them be themselves. You, too, might from time to time need to be affirmed, but that does not mean you lack anything. The completeness is there. You only need some confirmation of it. After a while, of course, you probably won't even need that.

I know this sounds vaguely Christian. In fact some of the psychologists I have mentioned will portray Christ, along with Buddha and others, as a fine example of B-love. Jesus was well advanced in the art of finding wholeness within, and He knew how to appreciate things. In this version of the gospel, Christ (if you will excuse the analogy) was something like Ferdinand the Bull who just sat and smelled the flowers and, for some inexplicable reason, was hauled off to the bull ring. Except for the bull ring part, which was a bad mistake, we ought to emulate Christ's way of loving. In other words, we should learn simply to be ourselves and give others the freedom and space to be themselves. Live and let live. That is love.

Christ's Kind of Love

That tidy picture of love is very appealing—especially to those who are more interested in having their freedom than they are in loving. It suffers the defect, however, of being wholly inaccurate in regard to Christ. Christ did not love in a liberal, nonpossessive manner. The Gospels, rather, give us a picture of a man of powerful passions who wept openly and threw people around bodily. It is difficult in places to avoid the impression of an impassioned lover: the kind of man willing to take rash action to win over his beloved, willing to make public scenes; willing to do almost anything short of tying her up and dragging her off.

At the same time, however, He is clearly the head. He will have things His way. There is no evidence that He is going to accept the bride as she is and leave her that way: "You must be perfect," He says. Instead of, "You are not in the world to live up to my expectations," He gives the impression that this is exactly why we are in the world. He seems to have the notion that He knows better than other people what is good for them. Clearly He has never heard of the nondirective approach. He tells a parable of a lord who throws a great feast. When the invited guests fail to arrive, the lord sends his servants out into the streets to bring in passers-by: "Make them come in," he commands.

I recite this catalog not to suggest that God in Christ suffers from need love—theologians tell us that is not the case—but to show that the kind of love He recommends to us by His example is the very opposite of what some psychologists would have us do. The one thing love cannot be is indifferent. It might be exacting, it might even be cajoling, but it cannot be blasé.

On these grounds, I think, we must be on our guard against some of what passes for love these days. Love, when it means building yourself up into the kind of person who is emotionally above it all, is not really love but self-flattery. And it is no compliment to the one you love. Who wants to be loved in a purely unselfish way, the object of a love that seems to want or need nothing we might give in return? We would like to feel that we are useful and not merely wards of charity.

Likewise, the kind of person who is full of sentiments and smiles and a largesse of love for all, but who basically cares no more for you than for the butterfly or the blade of grass, does you no favor. We much prefer to be preferred, singled out; we like to think our lover has been selective in his choice. Of course, need love can be carried to selfish and gluttonous extremes, but in ordinary life it is also a reflection of our condition as human beings. The fact is that we *are* needy; we *do* need to be completed. *Not* to feel need love may be a sign that we are seriously out of touch or else hardening into an unloving and unlovely creature.

Psychological Mistakes About Love

We do hunger and thirst, and that keenness will not be satisfied by anything within. We wouldn't tell a starving man to nourish himself on his inner food. Should we be telling the love-starved to love themselves with their inner love? Please understand, not all psychological advice on love is of this nature. Several excellent works on the subject (such as Rollo May's *Love and Will*) admit our needy natures. As a rule they will not admit our case to be quite as serious as Christianity makes it out, but there is at least what a Christian would call a realistic attitude.

For the sake of convenience these writers can be divided into two classes. The first class (the less sophisticated of the two) acknowledges that you are needy—so far so good—but then proceeds to make these needs the be-all and end-all of your existence. In reading these you get the impression that the first priority in a relationship is to have your needs met—if necessary you must demand they be met. This, in my opinion, is not much of an improvement over the idea that you don't need anyone. It reduces other people to need-fulfillers and makes relationships over into calculating affairs. This computational approach to love is not always mean-spirited, but it is altogether the wrong spirit. "Are my needs being met?" "Am I giving more than I'm getting?" "How much of my energies should I invest in a relation-ship?"

This attitude makes me think of the young man who came to look at my furnace boiler the other day. He had just taken a refresher course on home heating, and judging from his conversation, he seemed to think I ought to have nothing better on my mind than whether or not my furnace was operating at top efficiency, how BTU output compared to BTU input, did the attic have air leaks, how a new boiler would pay itself back in three years, how I could take advantage of an energy tax credit. His words buzzed around my head like flies. It was all very useful advice, of course, but I should not want this to be the ruling spirit of my domestic life, spending my watchful days with a caulking gun in one hand and a chart of interest rates in the other.

In the same way it is not unusual to meet men and women who seem to have just come from a course where all the energy coefficients of love have been figured out. They seem to have the idea that a relationship should be like a bookkeeper's balance sheet, as though a new wife ought to pay for herself in three years. They have a similar attitude to having children.

Common sense will tell us that life simply can't be reckoned like this; Christianity will tell us that it should not. There is suffering inherent in all love. Do what you will, you will not avoid it. Better to accept whatever fate God sends us than to lose the ability to love altogether—for that can easily happen once you approach love like this. Love requires a spirit of wholeheartedness not a spirit of strategic maneuvering.

We are all familiar with the second spirit, and we all take it with us into certain situations. You have probably experienced the frustration of wheeling your shopping cart up to the checkout lines of a crowded supermarket, only to find them all packed. You take up a position in one line but keep a watchful eye on the progress of the others. No need to stick with yours if another is moving faster. But you do not want to take that sort of tentative attitude into your married life no matter how many advise it. In that situation it is deadly and will surely wreck all.

The other class of writers (into which I would put Rollo May) is several notches higher. These psychologists write persuasively of the need to find a more mature love based on give and take, expecting the bad along with the good. They acknowledge the tragic element in love, and they emphasize commitment. What one is forced to object to in their work is not what is there but what is not there. There is sound analysis and sound advice, deeper understanding, better ways of relating. But there is no rationale for you to stay together if these fail to work. The question of why you should want to keep going on through thick and thin doesn't come up. It is simply assumed that for some reason you do.

The thing that is assumed, however, is that which makes all the difference. "Rationale" is really a poor word for it. I think "vision" is better; "a shared vision" better still. It is a fact of everyday observation that people who come together with a common goal or task, with a shared love for something outside each other—such as a choir or an outing club—have a more permanent bond than people who come together for the sake of coming together—such as an encounter group.

Chesterton said that "vigorous organisms talk not about their processes, but about their aims." "There cannot," he wrote in *Heretics*, "be any better proof of the physical efficiency of a man than that he talks cheerfully of a journey to the end of the world." It is when a man starts talking about his metabolism and heart rate that you wonder about his health. People in encounter groups do not plan journeys like people in outing clubs; rather, they talk about their processes: "How I feel about you" or "How I react when you say this about me." Well and good. But you cannot go on talking like that forever. It gets insufferably boring. And it is not good for a marriage when two people talk incessantly about their respective feelings. There are other things to do. A journey through life, however trite that may sound, is not a bad itinerary for a marriage.

Shared Memories

Perhaps something we said earlier about the importance of stories will be helpful in understanding the point. We said then that a life should be a story. For the same reasons we can say here that marriage ought to be a shared story: something to look forward to, something to look back on. It has been said that love is ninety percent memory. I am not sure of the percentage, but surely the pleasure of a story is doubled when you have someone to tell it to, particularly if that someone knows and loves the story as well as you do. One of the things that makes a love strong and lasting is shared memory: to be able to say, "Remember when?" Remember that weekend at the cottage? Remember that time we got lost in the Bronx? Remember that holiday in the mountains?

Now suppose instead you have reached middle age or older and there is no one with whom to share the story. There was that weekend at the cottage with A, but A drifted out of your life years ago. There was that time in New York with B, but B is married now and living elsewhere. There was that time in the mountains with C, but you have lost track of C. You are left then with a series of prefaces and perhaps the beginnings of some chapters. You might have had a story.

It is to this need for a vision and a shared story that Christianity can respond where psychology cannot. Appropriately, it responds with the story of a wedding—the story of Christ and His Bride. It is, says the church, the story you were born for. And though you may be old in years, you are still only in the early chapters of that book. Among all the voices that presume to instruct us about our lives, this one speaks with immeasurable comfort. For by a wise provision, so we are told, the Master of the feast has saved the best wine for last.

Sexual Love

One more topic needs to be addressed. A passage from Goethe will give us our point of departure. "Every cen tury," he wrote, ". . . tries to make the sacred common, the difficult easy, and the serious amusing—to which there really could be no objection if it were not that in the process seriousness and amusement are destroyed together." I said earlier that unless love and marriage are treated as sacred mysteries they do not work very well. It is hardly necessary to point out that in recent years they haven't been treated thus, and consequently they don't work well at all. We certainly can't lay the entire blame for this at the feet of psychology. But it does seem psychology has hastened the process. By their very nature the social sciences aim at the reduction of mystery: they are in the business of shining bright lamps into dark places. But not all things will come to light under those circumstances. A photo negative, as we know, will not: it needs a darkroom. Other things also suffer from overexposure to the glare, sex being one of them.

If one says nowadays that sex is sacred, one runs the risk of being ridiculed. But that is only because the job of demystification has been done so well. If someone managed to kidnap a princess, dressed her in rags and knocked her about the head so her speech was slurred, and then told his fellow thugs that this woman was a princess, they would likely not believe him.

Our society is in a similar situation with regard to sexual love. We find it difficult to see how anything that can be found in low places can also be found in the highest. Given the common and easily available state to which sex has fallen, it is not to be wondered at that the medical and psychological estimate would prevail: sex is not sacred at all. It is a natural thing, one more biological process among many. So let us eat and drink and sleep and have sex and be healthy.

Christianity won't go along with that. Neither did the

pagan world for that matter. The Greeks believed love was a
god and sex a goddess. The Romans felt that only virgins
should tend the vestal fire. In our better moments we don't
go along with the casual view of sex, either. We can see,
though not so clearly as before, that sex is something set
apart and not for the public realm, that what goes on behind
closed doors is not meant to go on the movie screen.

I think we may go further and say that even our natural
impulses reinforce this view. The sense of the sacred is
conveyed, among other ways, by reticence and the fact that
some things are not said—or said only with a sense of their
specialness. The fact that we tend to blush and stammer or
assume an awkward air of matter-of-factness when talking
about sex does not mean we are holdovers from puritanism
but simply that we realize the subject matter we are tackling
is not a purely biological phenomenon. No one, as far as I
know, ever blushed when telling children how grapefruit
should be eaten.

Unless you understand that Christianity considers sexual
love to be a sacred thing, you can never fully understand
why it insists that sex be set about with exclusions and re-
strictions. All sacred things are. It is not that it thinks sex a
bad thing but a high thing. Like other high things, it deserves to be bounded by objective rules and not wafted
about by gusts of changing emotion. The Christian position
on this is quite clear. Sexual love is too important to be left
up to spontaneity. The correctness of our sexual conduct
must not turn on the intensity of the moment's feelings but
rather on objective criteria: whether we have made a vow
and to whom. How else can it be? We are not allowed to
plead our case on the basis of, "It's all right if you're in love."
Much less on the defense, "It can't be wrong when it feels so
right." Poached trout, as John White points out in *Eros*

Defiled, tastes quite as delicious as the purchased kind, but it is still poached trout.

Finally, as with all things sacred, egalitarian ideas do not apply here. The sexuality of a wife is available only to her husband, and a husband's only to his wife. An invasion of sexual exclusiveness, such as rape, is rightly regarded as a kind of sacrilege. But even in less serious matters we ought to be able to see that sexual love cannot be divided up between this person and that without forfeiting its value.

Sex and Specialness

That brings us to the last point—the one made by Goethe. By their very nature some things cannot be made common without destroying what is good and worthwhile in them. In seeking to make certain desires easier to fulfill, you finally make them not worth having. Thomas Howard, in one of his books, points out that the specialness of certain places resides in their privileged setting. The beach we must walk miles to or the mountain lake set far back from the road has a peculiar charm and quality that is not given to a place of easy access and common traffic. Admission to such places can be had only under certain conditions. They are more appreciated because we have gone through the rugged initiation required to get there. But once these places are opened up as tourist spots with motels and billboards, refreshment stands and litter, their special quality departs.

We should not misjudge the intentions of social scientists and psychologists in regard to sex and marriage. They may find it impossible on scientific grounds to accept what must seem to them like primitive mumbo-jumbo—the mystery of sex, the Wedding Feast of the Lamb. They may honestly feel it is bad for us to labor under such superstitions. They may think it in our best interest to be led forward under banners marked "natural," "normal" and "well-adjusted." It is not an easy thing to judge intentions. But we do have a right to judge results. The result has been spiritual wreckage and human litter everywhere.

CHAPTER 16

The Larger Vision

This book set out to be a comparison of psychology and Christianity. It has not been a survey of all the types and kinds of psychology; its intention, rather, was to get at the spirit of psychology and beyond that to the climate of prevailing attitudes for which psychology bears a large responsibility.

By now you can see that the criticisms offered are not only criticisms of the psychological spirit but of the modern secular spirit as well, psychology being the most convenient representative of that wider attitude. The people who do the genuinely good work in psychology must forgive me for taking this wholesale approach. To draw the fine shades and distinctions between various schools and styles would necessitate several volumes.

Christian readers must also make allowances. They would be mistaken to conclude that psychology can now be safely ignored. If you pick carefully among the brambles, you will have sweet blackberries to reward you. Psychology does remind us of important things we all tend to forget—reminding us, for example, to pay attention to our children when they are good rather than waiting till they are bad; or reminding us that our behavior will be the model for theirs. We must remember as well that God can use any one of us to do His work: pastor, psychologist, social worker—even the thoroughgoing secularist who doesn't recognize or acknowledge Him. Still, the greater danger for Christians is not that they will miss out on the latest behavioral advice but that they will let their faith be confused with the prevailing spirit, whether psychological or secular.

That spirit has won many converts, mainly, I think, because it seems to promise something we are all looking for. It suggests a greater potential in life than the one we have lived up to: that the world is somehow better, wider, finer—or could be. Much of this book has been devoted to showing that that spirit is not what it presumes to be. Sometimes we hear that we live in a pagan society. But that is not so. Paganism was superior to secularism. It recognized, however dimly, that the world was governed from a sacred realm. Paganism was, as Chesterton said, the biggest thing in the world, until Christianity came, which was bigger. Everything since has been smaller.

The Misplaced Measure

Our present culture has been called "the psychological society." To us psychology seems like a big thing, but that is because we have misplaced the measuring stick. A husky boy seems large to his companions until he puts on his father's coat. Then he may appear merely ridiculous. If the psychological explanations of life and death, joy and pain seem impressive to us, it is because we have forgotten or never known how much larger the Christian explanation is. We speak glibly nowadays about the importance of the person, but only Christianity, it seems, is willing to draw him large as life, warts and all. Christianity is larger in the sense that a biography is larger than an application form, or as a novel catches the full character of a man where a case study cannot. It is full of the richness and detail of life as psychology is not.

It is larger also because it has a larger vision. We think of people as large-spirited in two senses. First, because they are full of charity, and second, because they have a large vision of life. This doesn't mean they have a rosy view, only one that takes more things into account. They see possibilities where others don't. They seem to have not a piece of knowledge but the whole, and thus the ability to put things in their proper places, making neither too much nor too little of them.

In the case of Christianity most people will concede that the charity is there but how about the vision? The average man who is not a Christian thinks of the faith as a gray, grim, affair. Popular psychology, by contrast, will often appear to him as a psychic liberator—an intoxicating, vine-clad Bacchus. This, I believe, is a mistake, the kind made by people who really know very little about psychology, and even less about Christianity. If you are looking for new worlds to explore, you had best look beyond psychology. It has the illusion of depth, but then so do facing mirrors, and I am afraid psychology is very much like one of those hall of mirrors you find in an amusement park. You get to see different facets and reflections of yourself, but that is all you see. A hall of mirrors is in reality only a room, and sooner or later you will want to find your way out. You will want to find a door.

At this point, of course, I am bound to remind you that Christ talked in exactly those terms: "I am the door; if anyone enters by me, he will be saved, and will go in and out and find pasture." That is decidedly not a message you will find in psychology. You don't have to believe it, but whether you do or not, you are hardly justified in calling Christianity the dull sister. If you are looking for new worlds to explore, you will need to find the door into them. Christianity has always claimed to have that door, and all the evidence suggests that it opens on a much wider vision than the rest of the world has imagined.

The Vision of Our Writers

I don't know how one proves this in a scientific sense, but there is certainly literary proof of it. You can take as an example the odd coincidence that binds together the work of George Macdonald, C. S. Lewis, G. K. Chesterton, and Dorothy Sayers. Macdonald and Lewis wrote fantasies and fairy tales—some of the best in the English language. Chesterton and Sayers wrote detective stories and mysteries—again, some of the best. Anyone who has read them knows that all these writers are capable of quickening the heartbeat or putting a catch in the breath. As you probably know, the coincidence that connects these masters of adventure and mystery is that all are also lucid and rational apologists for the Christian faith. They were as passionate about theology as they were about thieves or thistledown.

We could add a fifth. Tolkien, the Master of Middle Earth, never engaged in explicit apologies for Christianity, but he came close to doing so in his classic essay "On Fairy Stories" by suggesting that the Christian could through fantasy actually assist in the unfolding and enrichment of creation. The literary legacy left by these five suggests that we might be hasty in supposing that Christianity is incompatible with an unfettered imagination. Is it not much more likely to suppose that these writers could open worlds to us precisely because of the world that was opened to them?

Please notice that there is no parallel to this in the psychological imagination. No important psychologist, as far as I know, has ever written a romance, or a fantasy, or a fairy story, or an adventure. They study these things and comment on them, true, but that is where it ends. You could argue, of course, that Lewis and the others were born to the literary life. The point, however, is that the imaginative life and the Christian life can grow up together. We do not have much evidence of that in the psychological world. B. F. Skinner, the one important psychologist who wrote a novel, gave up his fiction writing almost before he began.

The Vision of Scripture

Of course, the Bible itself is glorious literature. It is a world of tyrants, traitors, friends, lovers, suppers, storms, and shipwrecks. Etched into every chapter of the Old and New Testaments is a record of smoldering jealousies, burning hatreds, and soaring loves: one man is sold into slavery by his brothers; another, in a fit of fury, dashes the sacred tablets to the ground; another lays down his life for his friends. That is the world the Christian imagination inhabits. It may not always be to our liking, but it is not dull. How small the world of id, ego, and super-ego—cramped within the confines of the skull—seems in comparison.

This is a theme on which many variations could be played, but I will choose just one more. The trouble with psychology is not that it incites our imagination and passions but that it finally deadens them. Take, for example, two poems about the experience of love, one representative of the psychological attitude, the other from the Psalms. It is interesting to note that both are considered prayers.

The first is "The Gestalt Prayer" of Fritz Perls which, judging from its one-time popularity, must represent the distilled wisdom of humanistic psychology on the topic of love:

I do my thing
And you do your thing.
I am not in the world to live up
    to your expectations,
And you are not in the world
    to live up to mine.
You are you and I am I,
And if by chance we find each other,
    it's beautiful.
If not, it can't be helped.*

The second prayer is from Psalm 42:

As a hart longs for flowing streams,
    so longs my soul for thee, O God.
My soul thirsts for God,
    for the living God.
When shall I come and behold
    the face of God?

The first seems to provide pragmatic guidelines for carrying on a relationship without getting tied down, yet it does not in any traditional sense have anything to do with either love or prayer. It is a paean to self-interest. One is forced to think of the "I" and "You" of the poem not as lovers or even friends, but as parties to a contract. The second prayer, the psalm, is at least recognizable to those who have been in love, as a love song. One need not be religious to understand the type of total commitment in this love.

Or consider some excerpts from The Song of Songs:

. . . he comes,
leaping upon the mountains,
    bounding over the hills.
My beloved is like a gazelle
    or a young stag.

*Copyright © Real People Press 1969. All rights reserved.

Behold, there he stands
   behind our wall,
gazing in at the windows,
   looking through the lattice.
My beloved speaks and says to me:
"Arise, my love, my fair one,
   and come away.

Set me as a seal upon your heart,
   as a seal upon your arm;
for love is strong as death,
   jealousy is cruel as the grave.
Its flashes are flashes of fire,
   a most vehement flame.
Many waters cannot quench love,
   neither can floods drown it.
If a man offered for love
   all the wealth of his house,
   it would be utterly scorned.

Perhaps the best comment that one can make about such ardent poetry is to repeat G. K. Chesterton's remark that "it is only too easy to forget that there is a thrill in theism."

But where, we must ask in all seriousness, is the thrill in me-ism? It does not readily spring to mind. The most that any self-help writer has said is that love is an important relationship skill. The most that any transactional analyst has said is that one ought to get strokes back for strokes given. The most that any psychological theory ever suggested is that love ought to be a reciprocated concern for the other's self-growth.

But that love ought to be a fierce loyalty and a consuming fire, a leaping heart and a longing search—that is something utterly outside the social sciences. It is the province of poets or prophets. When the Pharisee asks for the greatest commandment, Christ replies, "You shall love the Lord your God with all your heart, and with all your soul, and with all your mind, and with all your strength." This is perhaps an awesome demand, but it can in no way be construed as hostile to the passionate state of being. Passion is what it demands.

We are a world away here from the world of the Gestalt Prayer and the relationship experts. For someone schooled in the psychological tradition, the Christian counsel must appear as scandalous. "My whole heart?" "My whole strength?" Psychology is not comfortable with this kind of talk and wants frightfully to water the whole thing down to a more palatable formula. Some Christians will follow the psychological lead and do the same. Thankfully, most will not. Christians, after all, are romantics and would much prefer to take Christ for their bridegroom than the world.

The Vision of Your Self

Finally, what of your self—the thing psychology wants you to take so much trouble over and the thing Christianity urges you to let go of?

Christianity, as we know, demands humility. That is a hard course to steer when the rest of the world (and many Christian preachers with it) urges us in the other direction. But whatever can be said against humility, this much can be said for it: the humble person is in a much better position to enjoy life. He is, because he can still be surprised. He can take unexpected pleasure in life because anything he gets is more than he expected. "On practical grounds," wrote Chesterton in *The Defendant*, "the case for humility is overwhelming." It is the basis for appreciating the startling nature of stars and the tremendous nature of trees. It is the basis for falling in love. The lover's ecstatic conviction that "This is too good to be true" is just another way of saying that "This is too good to be happening to me."

The proud man, on the other hand, can never get much satisfaction because what he gets is always a little less than what he feels he deserves. It's not that good things don't come his way. It's just that when they do, he can't maintain any interest in them. His focus on himself crowds out the appreciation of what is not himself.

Bassanio's Choice

Remember how, in *The Merchant of Venice*, Bassanio must choose among three caskets to win the hand of Portia? One casket is gold, one silver, one lead. One contains the portrait of Portia and that, of course, is the leaden one with the inscription: "Who chooseth me must give and hazard all he hath." It's just the same with our faith. We are asked to hazard all, even self, for the sake of winning a better prize.

Inside the gold casket is a skull and the warning, "All that glisters is not gold"—a caution that seems appropriate for a society fascinated by gilded psychological promises.

The silver casket is inscribed, "Who chooseth me shall get as much as he deserves," and inside it is a picture of a fool's head. I need hardly say that this is the sort of choice the modern world encourages us in. And the prize seems very much the same.

Our choice, however, is more serious than Bassanio's. It is really the same choice offered to Adam and Eve: either we trust God or we take the serpent's word that we can make ourselves into gods. The temptation in the garden, which is the oldest of all seductions, never goes out of style.

Our selves, our hard-won self-image, our special plans and hopes, our pleasure—all these are very precious to us. If we lose these we fear we lose all. We do not wish to part with them any more than we wish to part with our children. But a parting is not always a disaster. And I imagine that like the parents of an overprotected child on his way to summer camp, we shall find our anxieties were not justified. If we take the camp director's advice and let him do the worrying, we shall have our child back at the end of summer, an inch taller, tanned and fit with a broad smile on his face and a more lovable disposition than we thought possible.

But that is a very poor suggestion of what the real case will be. There are many reassurances on that score: that he who loses his life shall find it, that we shall get all back a hundred-fold, that we shall be like Him.

Be like Him? But what does that imply?

Like Him

There is a curious problem at the beginning of Matthew's Gospel and also Mark's. I am sure you've come up against it. Our Lord says "Follow Me," and the apostles simply leave their nets and follow Him. We are tempted to wonder what else He said to them or what reasons He gave. Something seems to have been left out of the narrative.

What is left out, of course, is the immense strength of our Lord's personality. Ronald Knox gets to the heart of the matter in asking, "What was the magic of voice or look that drew them away, in those early days when no miracles had yet been done, when the campaign of preaching had not yet been opened? . . The tremendous impact which his force of character made on people—do you remember how, according to Saint John, his captors in the garden went back and fell to the ground when he said, 'I am Jesus of Nazareth?'—all that is difficult to realize in the Synoptists."[1]

The force of that personality is undiminished. Ages afterward, countless men and women still leave everything behind to follow Him. There is nothing in the annals of history to match that particular personality. Next to it, the psychological models of health and wholeness are dust and nonsense.

"True personality lies ahead," as Lewis observed, but this is the direction in which it lies. "It does not yet appear what we shall be," wrote Saint John, "but we know that when he appears we shall be like him."

Like Him. That is the kind of self that lies in store for us. Whatever self we have now is but the palest foreshadowing of true self. That is why the Greeks and Romans correctly perceived the soul to be feminine. Our souls receive personality from God. They are designed to be filled by Him. The danger for us all comes when we crowd them full of our own petty ambitions and our shortsighted ideas of fulfillment and leave no room for the work that must be done in us.

We shall be most ourselves when we become the self God intends us to be. And that, truly, will be a self to marvel at.

NOTES

Chapter 2

1. Stanislav Andreski, *Social Sciences as Sorcery* (New York: Penguin Books, 1974), pp. 25–26.
2. Ibid., p. 26.
3. Ibid., p. 29.

Chapter 3

1. C. S. Lewis, *The Problem of Pain* (New York: Macmillan, 1962), p. 41.
2. Ibid., pp. 59–60.

Chapter 4

1. C. S. Lewis, "Man or Rabbit?" in *God in the Dock* (Grand Rapids: Eerdmans, 1970), pp. 108–9.

Chapter 5

1. Will Schutz, *Profound Simplicity* (New York: Bantam, 1979), p. 9.
2. M. Scott Peck, M.D., *The Road Less Traveled* (New York: Simon and Schuster, 1978), pp. 270–71.
3. Even today it is interesting to note the relatively small space given in English bookstores to psychology. Self-help books are almost nonexistent.
4. G. B. Hill, ed., *Boswell's Life of Johnson*, vol. 2, revised and enlarged by L. F. Powell (Oxford: Oxford University Press, 1934–1950), pp. 260–62.
5. Henrik Ibsen, *Peer Gynt* (New York: E. P. Dutton, 1930), p. 163.
6. David Shapiro, *Neurotic Styles* (New York: Basic Books, 1965), pp. 77, 78, 87.

Chapter 7

1. Mircea Eliade, *The Sacred and the Profane,* trans. Willard Trask (New York: Harvest, 1959), p. 191.
2. Thomas Wolfe, *Look Homeward Angel* (New York: Modern Library, 1929), p. 493.

Chapter 8

1. Stanley Hauerwas, *A Community of Character* (Notre Dame: University of Notre Dame Press, 1981), p. 150.

Chapter 9

1. C. S. Lewis, *The Problem of Pain,* p. 146.
2. Thomas Howard, *The Achievement of C. S. Lewis* (Wheaton: Harold Shaw, 1980), pp. 38, 39.
3. J. R. R. Tolkien, *On Fairy Stories* in *The Tolkien Reader* (New York: Ballantine, 1966), p. 72.

Chapter 10

1. C. S. Lewis, *A Preface to Paradise Lost* (New York: Oxford University Press, 1961), p. 73.
2. Neil Postman, "Order in the Classroom," adapted from *Teaching as a Conserving Activity* (New York: Dell, 1979) in Fred Schultz, ed., *Annual Editions in Education 81/82* (Guilford, Conn: Dushkin, 1981), pp. 133, 134.

Chapter 11

1. Howard Kirschenbaum, *On Becoming Carl Rogers* (New York: Delacorte, 1979), p. 244.

Chapter 12

1. William R. Coulson, *Groups, Gimmicks, and Instant Gurus* (New York: Harper and Row, 1972) p. 99.
2. Three years after the break, the community was down to 280 members.

Chapter 13

1. Harry Blamires, *Where Do We Stand?* (Ann Arbor: Servant Books, 1980), p. 156.
2. Paul C. Vitz, *Psychology as Religion: The Cult of Self-Worship* (Grand Rapids: Eerdmans, 1977), p. 104.
3. David G. Myers, *The Inflated Self* (New York: Seabury, 1980), p. 143.
4. G. K. Chestérton, *Heretics* (New York: John Lane Co., 1905), p. 98.

Chapter 14

1. G. K. Chesterton, *Tremendous Trifles* (New York: Dodd, Mead, 1909), pp. 2, 3–4.
2. C. S. Lewis, *Surprised by Joy* (New York: Harvest, 1955), p. 238.

Chapter 15

1. Ronald A. Knox, *The Hidden Stream* (New York: Sheed and Ward, 1953), p. 224.

Chapter 16

1. Ronald Knox, *The Hidden Stream*, p. 107.

SELECTED BIBLIOGRAPHY

Andreski, Stanislav. *Social Sciences as Sorcery.* New York: Penguin Books, 1974.

Chesterton, G. K. *The Everlasting Man.* Garden City, N.Y.: Image Books, 1955.

Derrick, Christopher. *Sex and Sacredness.* San Francisco: Ignatius Press, 1982.

Gross, Martin. *The Psychological Society.* New York: Random House, 1978.

Hauerwas, Stanley. *A Community of Character.* Notre Dame: Univ. of Notre Dame Press, 1981.

Hitchcock, James. *Catholicism and Modernity.* New York: Seabury Press, 1979.

Howard, Thomas. *Chance or the Dance.* Wheaton, Ill.: Harold Shaw Publishers, 1969.

Lasch, Christopher. *Haven in a Heartless World.* New York: Basic Books, 1977.

Rieff, Philip. *The Triumph of the Therapeutic.* New York: Penguin Books, 1966.

Vitz, Paul C. *Psychology as Religion: The Cult of Self-Worship.* Grand Rapids: Eerdmans, 1977.